WHY GI͟R͟L͟S͟ ͟T͟A͟L͟K
—AND WHAT THEY'RE REALLY SAYING

A PARENT'S
SURVIVAL GUIDE
TO CONNECTING
WITH YOUR TEEN

**Susan Morris Shaffer
& Linda Perlman Gordon**

McGraw·Hill

New York Chicago San Francisco Lisbon London Madrid Mexico City
Milan New Delhi San Juan Seoul Singapore Sydney Toronto

SE

JUL 16 2005

The *McGraw·Hill* Companies

Library of Congress Cataloging-in-Publication Data

Shaffer, Susan Morris.
    Why girls talk and what they're really saying : a parent's survival guide to connecting with your teen / by Susan Morris Shaffer and Linda Perlman Gordon.
        p.   cm.
    Includes bibliographical references.
    ISBN 0-07-141786-9
        1. Parent and teenager.   2. Teenage girls—United States—Social conditions.
    3. Teenage girls—United States—Psychology.   4. Communication in the family.
    5. Communication—Sex differences.   I. Gordon, Linda Perlman.   II. Title.

HQ799.15.S525   2005
306.874—dc22   2004015257

Poem excerpt on page xviii from "The Seven of Pentacles," in *Circles on the Water* by Marge Piercy, copyright © 1982 by Marge Piercy. Used by permission of Alfred A. Knopf, a division of Random House, Inc.

Song lyrics on page 29 from "Do You Find Me Pretty?" by Tracy Carroll. Copyright © 2000 by Tracy Carroll. Used by permission.

    2 3 4 5 6 7 8 9 0   FGR/FGR   3 2 1 0 9 8 7 6 5

ISBN 0-07-141786-9

Interior design by Monica Baziuk

McGraw-Hill books are available at special quantity discounts to use as premiums and sales promotions, or for use in corporate training programs. For more information, please write to the Director of Special Sales, Professional Publishing, McGraw-Hill, Two Penn Plaza, New York, NY 10121-2298. Or contact your local bookstore.

This book is printed on acid-free paper.

To Arnie and Mark

Three books, two weddings, and 35 years of love and friendship

CONTENTS

ACKNOWLEDGMENTS

We are grateful for the generous support and encouragement we received for this project.

Thank you to our focus group parents and girls, who gave us invaluable personal stories throughout this project, especially to Sue Glick, Susan Fine, Barbara Moore, Lisa Trevino, and Maryanne Sandretti.

To Susan Wechsler, for her intelligence and insight and never being farther away than a telephone call.

To our colleagues, Sheryl Denbo and Phyllis Lerner, for their honesty and wise words and devotion to educational equity.

To Kimberly Lawrence Kol, for her wisdom and expertise, especially in the area of eating disorders.

To Susan Mikesell, for her many insightful contributions and support.

To our agent, Joelle Delbourgo, for her wise counsel, stimulating conversations, fabulous sense of humor, and exquisite professionalism.

To our editor, Judith McCarthy, at McGraw-Hill, for her vision, which became both the impetus and driving force behind this book.

To Kathy Dennis and the production team, also at McGraw-Hill, for making the book even better.

To Jean Bernard, for her impeccable attention to detail.

To Meryl Moss and staff, for their creativity, enthusiasm, and persistence.

To Ray Yau, for his vast knowledge of technology and ability to translate our ideas into a user friendly website.

To Judith Chused, Judy Bowles, and Carol Goldberg, for their inquisitive minds and inspiration.

To Jill Moss Greenberg and Linda Shevitz, who work every day to make all things possible for children.

To our siblings, Peter and Janine Perlman, Arlene and Bernie Ehrlich, Debbi and Dale Morris, and Eileen Zegar, for their constant enthusiasm and loving support.

Finally, as always, with all of our love, to our expanding families, Arnie, Zach, Emily and Dave, Mark, Seth, Elizabeth, and Josh.

INTRODUCTION

Life in the Balance

Parents are the most significant influence in a child's life.

Life with a 14-year-old girl can be compared to "wrestling with an octopus." For many of us who have survived these years, the dread of adolescence dominates any discussion about parenting, of boys as well as girls. Only after the ritual commiserating do we share the joys of adolescence. As the mother of a ninth grader said to us, "The compensation for living with adolescents is that they are very interesting." It takes perspective and understanding to appreciate the often puzzling, dramatic, and stressful times of these years for parents of millions of teenage girls. This was the state of parenting we found when we began to write this book about adolescent girls. We first wrote about raising adolescent boys, and in doing so, we discovered that despite the abundance of literature on the subject of raising girls, there was still a need for a discussion of the skills and tools we need to communicate and connect with our adolescent daughters.

In our book *Why Boys Don't Talk—and Why It Matters*, we examined the importance of connection in the lives of boys. Our objective was to share with parents the benefits of staying close to their sons, much as they do with their daughters. For parents of girls, our message is somewhat different. While it's important, of course, for parents of girls to stay connected to their daughters, we make a distinction between connection and enmeshment. While we ultimately value connection as a cornerstone of a happy life, we believe it is important to help our daughters to learn the value of what we call "engaged detachment" from the social messages of "what they ought to be" that inhibit the development of a healthy sense of self. This detachment will help them to develop a sense of well-being and self-sufficiency.

When we studied adolescent boys, we explored how easy it can be to become disconnected from boys and how limited their emotional lives can become if we are not careful. For adolescent girls, we discuss the ways we can help our daughters to broaden their circles and sense of themselves so that when connections with others in one sphere are in conflict, they have other spheres to turn to. We believe it is essential to encourage girls to appreciate their own competence, and we suggest ways that you as a parent can enhance that sense of capability.

Adolescent boys and girls are mirror images of each other. In general, boys learn to silence themselves in ways that diminish their understanding of their interior lives and emotional components. In general, girls are in touch with their emotional components but keep themselves from knowing or exposing their more complete, authentic selves—that is, a self that exists apart from their social relationships with any one group. For these reasons, boys "don't talk," and girls "do talk," and we are left trying to figure out what our adolescent sons and daughters are really saying. While the dynamics are different for boys and girls, the consequences are the same: they feel disconnected from their true selves and from their families. To minimize this occurrence, we have to provide adolescents with opportunities to develop emotional and moral courage.

As parents of both sons and daughters, all of whom were adolescents not so long ago, and as professionals in psychology and education, we bring to this project a unique combination of professional perspectives. We both work in gender, education, adolescent, and family issues—one of us as an educator and the other as a social worker. We have integrated our own personal and professional experiences with those of other parents and psychologists, educators, and experts who live and work with adolescent girls. In addition, we have reviewed the literature about adolescent girls in psychology, sociology, culture, education, and statistics.

Comparing our different experiences in raising our daughters and our sons, we have come to realize that although our girls have tended to share more information with us than our boys have, it has often been difficult to sort through the noise and accurately decode their intended messages. These are our goals for this book:

* To identify effective strategies for deciphering the necessary information from the drama of girls' daily lives
* To assist you as parents in developing skills to help your daughter establish a strong sense of self, while staying emotionally connected with her
* To strike a balance between the stereotypes of the "mean girl" and the "nice girl" so your daughter can create a sense of her authentic self
* To explore your own boundaries to avoid overidentification with and investment in the social successes and failures of your daughter

Exploring the Behavior of Girls

While researching the ways girls communicate and create connections, we developed a list of key questions:

* Why is it so much easier to learn the details of our daughters' lives than of our sons'?
* When our daughters share the myriad details of their lives, what are they really telling us?
* What is engaged detachment?
* What can parents do to facilitate the social development of girls?
* How do parents set boundaries between their lives and their daughters' lives so they can remain objective coaches?
* What skills do girls need to get through their adolescent years intact?
* What is important for parents to think about and to do during these formative years to help foster communication, connection, and the development of healthy and strong girls?

All of girls' behaviors deserve close exploration to find answers to these questions. Contradictions still exist. Sometimes girls may be more silent than talkative. For example, in the classroom girls may be quiet because they are self-conscious of being viewed as "goody-goodies" or teachers' pets. We need to help our daughters feel confident enough to articulate what they know without having to silence themselves. In order to help your daughter, you need to understand what goes on beneath the silence to decipher what she is really trying to express. Even though she may not always express herself with words, she still has many complicated feelings. What girls are saying is not always verbal; these feelings can also be demonstrated by their behavior.

Moreover, to understand the full landscape of girls' lives, we have to consider their experiences from various ethnic, cultural, racial, and socioeconomic backgrounds. We can't fall into the trap of lumping girls into one "female" category. One size does not fit all.

Using Fuzzy Logic for Parenting

Raising a child is a collection of parenting moments. The process doesn't follow the time frame for the scripted logic of a 30-minute sit-com, with the linear form of a beginning, middle, and end. Instead, parenting is more like the mathematical concept of "fuzzy logic," where uncertainties and discrepancies become clearer and more decipherable over time. An analogy is the archetypal discussion with kids about sex: one talk doesn't provide them with all of the information that they need to make responsible choices. It takes a collection of talks in response to different developmental needs and providing positive role models that help guide children to responsible decisions.

As parents, we have to provide many healthy messages over the span of our daughter's growing up and hope that she incorporates them into her perception of the world and herself and her decision making. Our job as parents is to communicate our values and beliefs, while separating our struggles from hers; to help our daughter heal when necessary; and to provide opportunities for her to develop what we call "a broader integrated identity."

A broader integrated identity is one in which a girl's sense of self is not completely dependent on any one interest or thing. Having a more expansive sense of self allows a girl to stay centered and more secure within herself in response to not being invited to a party, having less than stellar athletic skills, surviving a fight with a boyfriend, or not doing well on a history exam. These experiences are part of teenage life; everyone experiences some of them at one time or another.

Barbara, the mother of 22-year-old Alison, explained how she and her husband helped their daughter develop a broader sense of self in the face of academic difficulties: "Alison struggled so much with reading that in ninth grade they put her in special education classes in our large, urban high school. When we first discovered her dyslexia, we were relieved because the discrepancy between the bright girl we knew and the girl in the special ed classes finally made sense. The most important lesson that we learned during this period was that the only way to save her self-image was to find something other than school that she could excel in.

"For Alison it was dance. When she performed in front of an audience, she came alive. She was a different person: secure, confident, and creative. Alison lit up on the stage. This was an area where she could be competitive, and it provided her with another 'self' that she could rely on when she was feeling unsuccessful at school. The self-confidence that she gained from dance spilled over into other parts of her life, including, over time, doing well in school. She could draw upon her success in dance to help her define in a positive way who she was."

Alison's parents refused to let her be pigeonholed by only one facet of her life. They understood the importance of finding their daughter's passion and supporting her. The more opportunities we provide for our daughters to experience their own competence, the more resilient they become.

An important component to raising teenagers is being available to them. Staying close to your daughter may prevent risk-taking behaviors. The closer you are, the more opportunities you have to empower her. Contrary to the popular belief that little children need their parents more than adolescents do, we know that these years also require attentiveness and close supervision.

It is our intent to present parents with a practical guide to further understand the emotional dimensions of girls and increase the possibilities of competence and connection. What we learned from talking to many parents is that their desire to stay close to their children during the teenage years is universal. They just don't always know how (see Appendix A: "Positive Parenting").

Your family has operating principles and values that are unique to you and parenting styles that affect what works and what doesn't. We encourage you to be confident in teaching the principles and values specific to your culture and heritage. Helping your daughter develop a strong sense of self requires building confidence and pride in her heritage. Having self-confidence increases the resiliency of girls as well as their sense of well-being as they address the trials and tribulations of their age.

Often, you won't know in advance what specific methods will work with your daughter. However, by remaining engaged and constantly trying, you will become more knowledgeable about what works for her and when. Even with those strategies that do work, flexibility, variety, and a sense of humor are essential to getting through to your daughter during these demanding years. Don't despair; if you stay involved and stay connected during these years, you will also experience many precious moments.

You cannot tell always by looking
what is happening.
More than half a tree is spread out
in the soil under your feet.

—Marge Piercy, from "The Seven of Pentacles"

I

Understanding Your Daughter's World

WHY GIRLS TALK—AND WHAT THEY'RE REALLY SAYING

"Ophelia died because she could not grow. She became the object of others' lives and lost her true subjective self."

—MARY PIPHER, *Raising Ophelia*

In the words of the parents of a teenage daughter and son: "When our son, David, has a problem, we have to pry the details out of him with a crowbar, but every issue with our daughter, Amy, becomes a four-act melodrama that goes on and on." Unlike boys, who tend not to talk much with their parents, teenage girls provide an almost excessive amount of information about their daily lives. We have written *Why Girls Talk—and What They're Really Saying* to help you understand the complexities of teenage girls' lives.

Our girls' words as well as their behaviors reveal much about their inner lives. By providing insight into the culture of adolescence, we hope to help you to better understand your daughter so you can help her more accurately decipher and address her inner feelings. You may be able to prevent your daughter from spending her adult life sorting out childhood misconceptions and trauma. As one mother expressed it, "I want my daughter to figure it out earlier than I did."

Adolescence is a time of great stress for parents and children. To parent girls effectively during this period, you must deal with several complex matters, such as sources of girls' emotional vulnerabilities, the damaging impact of the media portrayal of beauty as the defining element of personal worth, the factors that influence girls' self-esteem, and the impact of friendships and peer pressure. We provide effective techniques for you to address these issues.

Although our society encourages boys and girls to be autonomous and to pursue individual accomplishments, girls also are taught that forming and sustaining relationships is of major importance. More than boys, girls are expected to reconcile these two—often conflicting—definitions of success. We discuss psychological theory and popular literature to explore these issues, and we identify a road map for parenting teenage girls. As quoted in Jo Ann Deak's, *Girls Will Be Girls*, one mother describes her difficulty in developing an effective game plan: "I'm not saying that being a parent has ever been easy, but my parents had much more clarity about the world . . . and society supported them. There's just no script anymore."

The Paradox of Aggression

Girls' behavior is driven primarily by the expectation that they must behave cooperatively. Their behavior reflects a strong emphasis on collaboration and acceptance by their family, other adults, and, especially, their peers. They are also motivated by their fear of rejection and isolation. Girls' culture is based on both cooperation and social manipulation. It does not permit them to be in touch with and/or display how they really feel, e.g., angry, disappointed, proud, or frustrated. The resulting unexpressed and unprocessed feelings can create inner rage.

We used focus groups of teenage girls and their parents to conduct our primary research (see Appendixes B and C for focus group questions). We learned about two critical factors of teenage girls' development: the tremendous power of peer groups and the reluctance of girls to express anger (or their true feelings) in a direct manner. Whereas boys tend to display their teenage angst through overt acts of physical aggression, girls tend to express this same painful struggle in ways that are subtle, masked, and difficult to identify or interpret.

Our observations confirmed those of others. According to Phyllis Chesler in *Woman's Inhumanity to Woman*, social manipulation is an "indirect aggression [that] is carried out in order to harm the opponent, while avoiding being identified as aggressive. . . . Indirect aggression is akin to a voodoo hex, an anonymous but obsessive act in which the antagonist's soul, more than her body, must be got at, must be penetrated, must be nullified."

Girls don't lash out to be malicious; it's the only acceptable tool they have to process their aggression. They lash out to protect themselves because girls don't feel that they have permission to say what they really want, especially if this is different from what they think is expected of them. By molding their personality to fit the group, girls internalize the social pressure to be cooperative.

In our book *Why Boys Don't Talk*, we observed that boys who lack a full range of affiliations and emotional expressiveness often turn to competitive models defined by winning or losing. Competition is one of the few acceptable models for expressing their emotions. Girls also feel pressure to restrain and hide their true feelings, which greatly limits their available options for healthy self-expression, including frustration and anger. The lack of acceptable outlets can be devastating for

---

"Many people think of adolescence as a stage where there is so much peer influence that parents become both irrelevant and powerless. . . . Parents are just as important to adolescents as they are to smaller children."
—DONNA WALKER JAMES and GLENDA PARTEE,
No More Islands: Family Involvement in 27 School and Youth Programs

girls. Unfortunately, they frequently hide their difficulties and resulting rage from parents and other adults. In "Words Can Hurt Forever," James Garbarino and Ellen deLara observed that, "Teachers and other school personnel often observe adolescent anger, but they typically don't see the profound feelings of helplessness and hopelessness that underlie much of this anger."

Girls use social manipulation to try to control their universe. Generally, this involves complex interactions to indirectly control events. These practices are based on the belief that to be assertive is to be forward or pushy; fear that self-assertion may result in being labeled as not a team player; and worry of appearing emotional and/or hysterical. Girls' manipulation practices take many forms, including covert behaviors to get back at someone, such as talking behind her back, being passive-aggressive, and playing the peacemaker.

Anyone who has ever worked or lived with teenage girls knows how much drama exists in their everyday lives. In addition to reacting to their raging hormones, this drama is the result of their need for validation. Girls need feedback from others before they can internalize a sense of well-being. The drama is really a girl's verbalization of her feelings in a manner that she believes will produce a validating reaction.

We have to work to understand the message behind the drama. In most instances, girls are wrestling with the difficult problems of defining themselves and their relation to others. Is it OK to step out of the group? Is it OK to disagree with the group's consensus? Can I stand out as an individual and still be a member of the group? Girls must answer these questions to develop their own identity.

Girls suffer from a constant tug-of-war between their need to individualize and their need to establish group identification. In contrast, boys define themselves independently, often by rejecting anything they perceive to be "feminine" or "soft." Boys don't talk about their feelings because they think it's safer not to talk. Boys think they are cool by appearing to disengage. Girls hope to be cool by being engaged and accepted by the group. We all know girls talk, but the words may not match who they really are.

You have an opportunity to influence your daughter's development. Take time to listen through the noise, with caution and care, and focus on your daughter's real needs. This can help you to gain greater clarity and purpose when addressing your daughter's identity issues. Your insight will help to establish her sense of self. Your daughter's accurate self-knowledge can protect her from subsuming herself into the girl she thinks she is supposed to be or what her friends think she should be. We need to teach our daughters how to identify the underlying issues of self-definition that drive their emotions, just as we teach our sons to understand and articulate the language of feelings. Without these skills, boys and girls struggle with knowing themselves and using their own voices.

By helping your daughter to sort out the wheat from the chaff, you enable her to interpret what the real issues are. "I hate you" may really mean "I'm scared that if I don't have a later curfew my friends may think I'm a baby." When you first begin to suggest what's really going on, your daughter may protest because the concept is new to her and it may make her uncomfortable. For example, she may not want to go to a particular party but may feel she has to go or lose face. Helping your daughter to figure out what *she* wants, rather than going along with the group, is essential to her developing effective decision-making skills.

Patience is essential. Planning a Friday evening with a teenage girl is more difficult than planning the invasion of Normandy. Between the time she gets home from school and "show time," your daughter's plans can change countless times. One mother of a 15-year-old daughter remarked, "I never say yes or no to the first requests. I used to take each request seriously, until I realized that I could avoid numerous battles if I just waited until the last moment to give permission for or against."

Strong emotions often mask underlying pain and confusion. In the midst of such chaos, try to figure out what is really important to your daughter, what she wants to do versus what she thinks she should do, and what she really feels about herself, school, family, and friends.

Amy, the mother of 15-year-old Nicky, commented, "Sometimes I see Nicky acting silly so she can feel a sense of belonging to her group. I know she doesn't care about some of the things they discuss . . . yesterday she pretended to like the Dixie Chicks, when she doesn't. I think she subjugates her own ideas and thoughts to belong." As a result of the inaccurate messages our daughters give out, much of what we hear doesn't give us the information we need to make good parenting decisions. We often are presented with a puzzle that we must work to translate.

Once they become adolescents, girls think we parents become dumber by the minute. At the same time, they want our approval. Even though adolescents perceive their parents to be Neanderthals, we must persevere. As Mark Twain reminds us, "When I was a boy of 14, my father was so ignorant I could hardly stand to have the old man around. But when I got to be 21, I was astonished at how much the old man had learned in seven years."

The Sum of All Fears

Anger can be a major concern because of the underlying rage that many girls experience. In our focus groups, a mother told us about her daughter's struggle with explosive anger. Her daughter, Stacey, asked for a new sweatshirt. When her mother said it wasn't necessary with summer coming on, Stacey flew into a fit of rage. She lashed out verbally and even smacked her mother. Stacey's mom had long been worried about similar outbursts. The next day, during a quiet moment, the mother tried something new. Rather than angrily criticizing Stacey's conduct, the mother gently prodded her. She sat next to her, put her arm around Stacey, and asked her why the sweatshirt was so important.

With this encouragement, Stacey revealed that the girls in her peer group had been taunting her for being "fat." She explained that the sweatshirt was her way of hiding her body. Stacey desperately wanted to avoid being picked on and felt overwhelmed when her mother said no. Stacey's rage at her mother was an expression of her embarrassment about her body. "Buy this for me" actually meant "Help me."

This mother taught herself how to use direct, gentle, supportive communication to explore the underlying cause of her daughter's outburst. By not getting caught up in the words, she could hear from Stacey's voice that something else was going on. Once Stacey became convinced that her mother heard and understood her, she was receptive to learning more socially appropriate ways to express her feelings of frustration. Eventually, Stacey and her mom became very effective at communicating, often with a mere glance or eye message. This breakthrough created a trusting and satisfying relationship.

Her mother taught Stacey tools for assessing her internal feelings, which helped Stacey to solve her problems more effectively. As Stacey learned how to manage her problems more effectively, her frustration diminished. Stacey's self-esteem was boosted because she subsequently felt good about how well she could handle her anger.

Girls sometimes express their concerns about themselves and their developing sense of self by adopting nonconforming behaviors. In our focus groups, a mother shared with us her experience with her daughter who always tried to look different (purple hair, grunge clothes). At first, her mother was proud of her daughter's individuality. But as her daughter became more and more socially isolated, the mother realized that she looked different from other kids because she felt "different." The mother was clueless about what to do. She was reluctant to share her concerns with other parents because she was embarrassed that her daughter didn't fit in. She was afraid others would judge her to be a failure as a parent. This mother would be comforted to learn that other parents have similar concerns.

Girls also react to peer concerns by using compensation techniques to mask the true reasons for their behavior. One mother labeled this conduct, the "veil of paranoia." While girls may communicate many details of their lives, they also mask their feelings to protect themselves from criticism. According to *Woman's Inhumanity to Woman*, girls often come to believe that there is "danger in authentic encounters," and learn how not to disagree in direct or confrontational ways.

Samantha, a self-assured 13-year-old, told us that she made the mistake of speaking the truth once and learned the unfortunate lesson that honesty can really backfire: "My best friend, Kristin, asked me whether I liked her new jeans, and I told her that I thought they were cheesy and trendy. Because we always check in with each other about clothes, I assumed that she would want to know how I really felt. But the second the words slipped out of my mouth, I wished I could swallow them. Kristin looked like she was about to cry and asked me how I could say such a thing. She didn't talk to me for days, and it practically took me crawling on my knees to get her to forgive me. I had no idea that she had saved her baby-sitting money to buy these designer jeans.

"Now when anyone asks my opinion, I keep the bad stuff to myself and say, 'That's great, they're really cool!'" Samantha's experience demonstrates how girls learn to keep their more controversial opinions to themselves. However, if Samantha knew how to express herself more diplomatically, the outcome may have been different. Because Samantha didn't have these skills, she learned it was safer to withhold dissenting opinions and her true feelings.

Complex Interactions

There is much to learn about the environment in which girls live. We have to be careful not to stereotype our daughter's friendships or to put her into a certain category or box. The terrain can be rough for even the most popular girl, and understanding the landscape and how it affects your individual child is paramount. We can take nothing for granted when raising a teenage girl. Rejection and isolation are traumatic, and they can be destructive if you don't intervene when your daughter is behaving like a bully or is being victimized. However, your first reaction must be to carefully listen to your daughter in order to understand her life.

In our focus groups, we have observed that girls experience social exclusion as devastating because they define themselves in relation to their peer group. Leslie, the mother of a 13-year-old, tells the following story: "My daughter, Sarah, was invited to a Friday night sleepover. She had swim practice early the next day, and she knew that it was important to get enough sleep. She is usually OK about coming home at a reasonable time, but this time she went ballistic. Sarah's reaction didn't match the content, and I knew something else was going on. Finally, she told me that a group of friends were spending the night and if she wasn't there, she could be their next victim. Sarah actually said, 'Mom, they'll kill me off if I'm not there to protect myself.'

"I really didn't know what to do. If she spent the night, practice would be rough, but she seemed so vulnerable that I didn't want to put her 'in harm's way.' I let Sarah make the choice. She decided to spend the night but wanted to be picked up early enough to go to swim practice. Sarah was so appreciative of me letting her make the decision. This incident gave us a good opportunity to talk about the meaning of friendship, while at the same time learning how to watch your back. I wouldn't want to be 13 again!"

In one of our focus groups, another mother said, "The horrible treatment some girls inflict on others creates scars that can't be seen." This observation is supported by the recent literature. In *Odd Girl Out*, Rachel Simmons states that bullying among girls is epidemic. Rosalind Wiseman, in *Queen Bees and Wannabes*, argues that if a teenage girl is rejected by one of the popular girls, she may become a victim for good.

Many mothers told us stories about their daughters' rejection by friends. One mother could hardly console her 16-year-old daughter, Maggie, after her friends accused her of liking someone else's boyfriend. Girls tend even to fight cooperatively. The group's wrath was fast and furious. In this age of instant messaging and e-mail, the attacks against Maggie spread throughout her peer group in less time than it takes parents to make a phone call. Maggie's social environment became so negative that she didn't want to go to school.

Maggie's pain was real. Without acceptance by her group, she felt a loss of her identity. Mistakes happen. Unfortunately, sometimes with groups of girls a mistake is viewed, as one 13-year-old girl described, "as if I killed somebody." During these terrible events in their lives, girls need our perspective and patience. We must take their pain seriously. You can begin the process of healing by teaching your daughter the social skills necessary to defend herself when her peer group attacks her. We should expect our daughters to learn from their mistakes and, at the same time, let them know we will help them through that process. Parents can use these group attacks to teach their daughters not to engage in the same conduct. Your daughter has to depend upon you to be rational and to tell the truth. If she was wrong, tell her and help her to repair the damage. To be most helpful, it's important that you understand the context your daughter is operating in and the tremendous pressure she may feel to conform to her peers' expectations.

Another mother described how "Girls mentally break each other down. . . . Girls choose sides, which can ruin someone's whole year; trust me, I know. They confess intimate feelings. They know each other's weak spots and go for them when they get angry." Jessica, a 17-year-old senior, recalled, "Middle school is all about ganging up, who can get more people to get their back. They mostly make fun of someone's physical appearance or whatever they know about a friend's insecurities." When girls are on the receiving end of this behavior, for many "the threat of disruption of an affiliation is perceived not just as a loss of a relationship but as something closer to a total loss of self," according to Jean Baker Miller's *Toward a New Psychology of Women*. While teenage boys practice physical fighting to assert their individuality, girls practice fighting for a definition of self through social behavior.

Parents told us stories about their girls being harassed or socially ostracized from female peer groups because of a seemingly minor relationship infraction. Whatever the offense, the punishment always exceeds the crime. The response is so punitive to remind the "perpetrator" of the principal value of cooperation. The underlying assumption here is that an infraction against one is an infraction against the group. This type of harassment is multicultural; as Phyllis Chesler says, "Girls of all colors have their own ways of bullying and beating each other." Many parents dismiss this behavior as "girls will be girls." This is a major mistake. Give your daughter the clear message that harassing behavior is never appropriate.

The Relational Code: Breaking Away

We offer our daughters the most powerful role models for relationships. This enables us to help them to learn to recognize and master their own feelings. We can teach our daughters, by example, that disagreements between friends and colleagues are normal and can be worked out without any permanent injury. Like every other skill, problem solving in relation to friendships is a learned behavior. Once again, you are your daughter's best teacher.

Joanne related a story about a confrontation with a friend and the lesson she and her 15-year-old daughter, Lily, learned from it. At dinner, Joanne told her husband, Robert, about how her friend Carol always made sure to put her mat right in the middle of the front row, blocking Joanne's view of the instructor during their yoga class. Thinking this was funny, and clueless about the repercussions, Robert told Carol's husband, John, that this habit annoyed Joanne. Of course, John went home and said something to Carol, who was humiliated about being talked about behind her back and was furious with Joanne. Joanne was mortified when Carol called to chew her out. Lily heard the conversation.

Because the relationship with Carol was important to her, Joanne worked hard to come to some understanding about what happened and how to fix it. Joanne acknowledged that by being so indirect, she behaved like an adolescent. Once Carol and Joanne had discussed what happened, they reached an understanding and laughed about it.

When Joanne got off the phone, she used this incident as a "teachable moment." She said to Lily, "My mistake is a good lesson for both of us. It's really important to be straight with people you care about and to admit when you're wrong." If they had not worked to resolve their issue, Carol and Joanne would have confirmed the validity of teenage conduct. This would have been the wrong message to give Lily.

Relationships are of paramount importance to girls. To address issues of self-worth, in addition to social manipulation, girls also engage in self-protective insincerity. This insincerity may shield them from group criticism, but it also serves to deny their talents, motivations, intent, and opinions. Girls who fall into this type of behavior are particularly vulnerable because, if their peers devalue them, they tend to have no inner sense of self to rely on. We call this phenomenon the "relational code." Everything is subsumed by the relationship. Girls allow the group to hold their self-esteem. Friendship becomes bigger than anything else. Expressing pride in their own achievements causes them to be susceptible to rejection and the loss of friends. To protect themselves, many girls develop an almost perverted modesty about their accomplishments, which can produce misplaced self-doubt. In adult women, this behavior pattern has been called "the impostor syndrome."

Girls tend to rely on the group for their sense of self in a different way than boys do. A boy's group status is likely to be the result of performance—for example, athletics. A girl's sense of self is tied to her cooperation with and/or contribution to the group. Because they are expected to subordinate their needs to the needs of the group, girls are reluctant to appear too powerful or independent. Traditionally, a girl's group status is, in part, based on more subjective criteria, such as popularity, style, personality, and looks. A girl's sense of self is built on her relationships with others, interdependence, emotional connectedness, and being responsive to the needs of others. Lyn Mikel Brown and Carol Gilligan in *Meeting at the Crossroads: Women's Psychology and Girls' Development* refer to this need to subjugate oneself to the group as the "tyranny of niceness."

Girls are often judged by how giving they are toward others and their nurturing capacities. According to Louise Erdrich, as quoted in Teresa Wiltz's "Louise Erdrich: The Latest Installment," "Women either go along with things, in a nice way, as I was taught to do, and make people happy and try to be the all-forgiving goddess, or you break out of it and are yourself, with every failing and every strength. You can't expose your strengths without exposing your failings as well." You can best teach your daughter to acknowledge and express her true self by sharing your strengths and weaknesses.

Importance of the Authentic Parent

Identifying and expressing emotions builds emotional intelligence. Do not be afraid to verbalize your own range of emotions, including anger, disappointment, sadness, frustration, happiness, and joy. Daughters who see these expressions as a normal part of living are less afraid to explore their own full range of emotions. Positive relationships can withstand, if not benefit from, strong emotions. Through healthy emotional expressions, girls can better identify and cope with their feelings.

Recapturing your own memories can help tremendously in making sense out of your daughter's adolescent misunderstandings. Thirty to forty years later, mothers in our focus groups still could feel the pain of teenage rejection. Laura, the mother of two teenage daughters, recalled the blow to her self-esteem when she was "dumped" at summer camp: "I went to summer camp for many years. During a game of jacks, when I was 13, my [ball] rolled underneath the filthy, dust-laden bunk bed of my friend Barbara. I laughed at all the junk Barbara stored under her bunk, and she cried. Before I realized what was happening, two other bunk mates came to Barbara's defense. When we were going to breakfast the next day, nobody in my bunk would walk with me to the flagpole. I knew I was in trouble."

Laura described this experience as if it had happened yesterday. The focus group could see the pain on her face, and this enabled them to understand why girls have difficulty establishing their self-esteem without the assistance of a caring adult. Such incidents in your daughter's life may seem minor until you remember your own experiences. Because girls relinquish much of their sense of self to belong to a peer group, every incident is a potential assault to their self-esteem. You can contribute to a solution only when you spot the problem. You can affirm your daughter's sense of self-worth with genuine praise and honest feedback. In all likelihood, your daughter will not immediately internalize your message that she will be fine, have close friends, have happiness, and be fulfilled again. But over time, your supportive voice will resonate within her. She will consider these messages in her decision making and estimation of self-worth.

We offer one important caveat. Many parents remark how often they get heavily involved in the drama, only to be the last to know when everything is OK again. Try not to become overly invested in your daughter's drama and take the hurt personally. Your role is to be an objective coach for your child, as hard as that may be, not to relive adolescence through her. Ellen, the mother of 14-year-old Alexa, explained, "I'm real careful not to overreact to the insults and hurts, because I know that this magnifies their impact on Alexa. I just need to keep it real, keep a cool head to try to contain the impact of the drama. If I take it personally, it becomes my issue as well as Alexa's issue. That's not helpful for her."

Don't expect to be thanked regularly for your help or to be apprised of progress or closure of an episode; your daughter's behavior will demonstrate when she has resolved her issue. The important point here is to remain a supportive adult who neither minimizes nor overexaggerates the significance of an event or feeling. This balance teaches about authentic relationships.

Understanding the intricacies of teen friendships is a key to helping girls to successfully navigate adolescence. You provide the necessary security and safety during this turbulent period, so you should demonstrate to your daughter the benefits of coming to you. By doing so, you will build a healthier connection with her. Remember, you are your daughter's parent, not her best friend. Unfortunately, if you take your role as parent seriously, sometimes your daughter may not "like" you. This comes with the territory.

"We Can Work It Out"

Peer groups notwithstanding, you influence your child greatly. You must teach your daughter constructive ways to voice her concerns. You should try to help her to develop the ability to acknowledge her sense of self and to understand group dynamics. Help your daughter to "hold" or be responsible for her own identity by providing her with honest reflection—not grandiose praise—and unconditional love. Constructive criticism is easier to hear from you than from her peers.

Providing your daughter with opportunities to develop a fully integrated identity will assist her in building more realistic relationships with appropriate boundaries. By encouraging your daughter to be aware of the dynamics of conforming behaviors, you can help her to understand why girls have difficulty affirming themselves within a group. Boys toot their own horns. Girls rely on the group to do this for them. A girl may say, "I'm not good at that," and wait for the group to respond, "Oh yes you are." If a girl does well on a test, she may say, "I was lucky," and a boy may say, "I nailed the test."

To parent effectively, you need tenacity and patience; unfortunately, it is easy to lose focus. You should expect to be in a state of watchfulness during the decade-long period of adolescent development. Your job is to try to make it go better over time. Think long term. You need to teach girls how to make amends when they are wrong, how to construct better solutions, and how to rebound from disappointments and hurts. In addition, as Marianne in Judy Mann's *The Difference: Growing Up Female in America*, said, "I realize I can give her something other than love, which comes with virtually no thought, no judgment, no holding back. I can also give her admiration and respect for how she thinks and how she handles herself."

Girls face a dilemma that requires you to practice and perfect fancy footwork. Many girls feel responsible for taking care of the needs of others before their own, making the voices of friends louder than their own internal voice. When girls fail at being good caretakers, they have feelings of self-doubt and self-deprecation. You should validate the benefits of caring and connection but resist your daughter's abandonment of her individual spirit and vitality. Last, it's helpful to turn to your own friends for support during these frequently turbulent years. Parenting teens gives the expression "It takes a village to raise a child" a whole new meaning.

DEVELOPING YOUR DAUGHTER'S PERSONAL COMPASS

The following assessment will help you to gauge to what degree you are being successful at assisting your daughter to develop her own sense of self. For example, if your daughter is able to own her mistakes and make amends, she will have healthier relationships with other people.

Indicate by circling a number between 1 and 5 if you agree or disagree with the following statements; 1 indicates strong agreement, and 5 indicates strong disagreement.

I teach my daughter to develop her identity by:	Strongly Agree				Strongly Disagree
Encouraging her to participate in more than one group of friends	1	2	3	4	5
Valuing her individual opinions	1	2	3	4	5
Listening and coaching rather than doing for her	1	2	3	4	5
Communicating the importance of owning her own mistakes and making amends	1	2	3	4	5
Providing her opportunities to problem solve	1	2	3	4	5
Preparing her to cope with disappointments	1	2	3	4	5
Strengthening her ability to empathize with others	1	2	3	4	5
Enabling her to identify and understand the underlying sources of her emotions	1	2	3	4	5

Golden Girl

Tyranny of Beauty and Culture

"Media leaders can take pride that they portray many women as intelligent problem solvers, but they should also be aware of how often they just paint a pretty picture."

—LOIS SALISBURY, President, Children Now

The definition of womanhood has varied over time and among cultures; however, beauty remains one of the principal standards. In contemporary America, the women's movement and economic necessity have expanded the definition of womanhood to include competence in the business world and independence. Teenage girls struggle with these sometimes competing standards of beauty and capability. Currently, girls are required to live up to both sets of expectations. In contrast, when it comes to physical appearance, boys live in less of a straitjacket. Humor, competence, and success can trump looks, giving boys a more acceptable range of ways to fit in.

Research by Lois Salisbury reported in *Reflections of Girls in the Media* demonstrates that the media and culture play powerful roles in shaping attitudes and perceptions of teenage girls. She says that adolescent girls spend more than 20 hours a week watching television, during which time they see 20,000 advertisements a year. They listen to CDs and the radio, read fashion and teen magazines, watch music videos, play video games, and go to the movies.

These "spectator sports" are among the most influential forces in the lives of girls. A 16-year-old sophomore, Stephanie, told us, "A girl can be anything . . . as long as she is thin and pretty." No matter how much has changed for girls, this attitude is part of the idealized folklore of modern femininity. "Pretty" is *the* standard by which girls are judged, and the media promote this tyranny of beauty.

Hour after hour, American girls receive powerful signals to be thin, beautiful, and sexy. For example, at the 2003 Oscars, host Steve Martin said, "A movie star is tall, short, thin, and skinny." The messages about what is considered to be beautiful are both subtle and blatant. In the past 30 years, the idealized woman has shrunk from Marilyn Monroe's size 12 to Courteney Cox Arquette, who appears to be no bigger than a size 2.

The narrow standards for how girls should look and act (blond, thin, tall, big breasts, long legs, straight hair, trendy clothes, tanned and smooth skin) are communicated through popular culture, parents, and other girls. As girls develop into young women, many of them struggle to attain a body type that nature never intended them to have.

"It is vital to the survival of the beauty, fashion, and diet industries that women believe that their hair, clothing, body shape, and weight are inadequate. The economy would have much to lose if women accepted themselves, 'flaws' included."
—NAOMI WOLF, "Hunger"

You must ask yourself how you can protect your daughter from this onslaught of unrealistic body images and diminish their impact on self-esteem. What can you do to expand girls' definition of beauty? There's nothing intrinsically wrong with girls trying to look the best they can. The problem begins when girls damage their physical or psychological health in the impossible pursuit of an unattainable marketed perfection to be thought of as acceptable.

Preoccupation with physical appearance is about fitting in. Teenage girls believe that looking a certain way provides them access to the right group and opportunities for relationships with boys. Reliance on external feedback is, unfortunately, only a temporary fix and does not sustain self-confidence. Nevertheless, the "appearance" of what good looks and a pretty body provide is so powerful for girls that it can undermine their individuality and competence.

Narrow standards of beauty make teens feel they don't measure up. From childhood through mature adulthood, girls and women feel pressure to conform to society's ideal of feminine beauty. Regardless of their weight or body type, there were virtually no adult women with whom we spoke who were satisfied with their bodies. Feelings of inadequacy are now starting with girls as young as 10 years old. Glynn, 16, said, "I think about how I look all the time. I always want to look like the girl on the magazine cover, whether it's Reese Witherspoon, Jennifer Lopez, Britney Spears, or Halle Berry."

These exceptional examples of beauty have created impossible standards. This inability to match society's vision of girls leaves millions of them feeling inadequate, often causing eating disorders and other psychological challenges. Food is one of the few things they can control. Adrianne, a 15-year-old freshman, explained, "When I went into a new high school, I wanted desperately to be part of things. Everyone looked thin to me, so I thought if I had a better body, people would like and accept me."

The absurdity of this ideal became clear when before one of our focus groups, we found ourselves seated at a kitchen table next to a male college student who was poring over his sister's latest issue of

Bazaar magazine. Unprompted by his sister or us, he was stunned by the images he saw and said:

> The women in this magazine look like they stepped off a Barbie Doll assembly line. They are perfectly molded and sculptured pieces of art—not people. Art without the merit of creation is eye candy! Is this what women want to be? High heels—those can't be comfortable. Are they sexy? Yeah, but that's not what makes it for me. Why the overkill? These magazines create the illusion that this exaggeration [three-inch stiletto heels] is necessary. This is garbage. Your uniqueness is what is necessary. You need to set yourself apart, because you're never going to [live] up to these standards.

What is so powerful about this unsolicited description is how surprised the boy was at the pressure girls feel to look a certain way and his understanding of how impossible this goal is. It's no wonder generations of women seek irrational means to look a certain way. Meeting this ideal can't be done without the airbrushes and filters that make emaciated bodies look perfect. The results leave girls and women feeling bad about their bodies no matter how thin or disciplined they are.

Ballet is particularly punishing when it comes to body image. Barbara, the mother of 18-year-old Becky, said, "I really couldn't believe it when Becky came home from ballet and said, 'Mom, Amy and I are the only girls who sweat, and my teacher told us to lose a little weight.' This was horrifying to hear, especially because Becky had always been pretty slender and Amy was average size. I was outraged. I try hard to counter the images on TV and magazines by telling my daughter how unrealistic they are. And now her ballet teacher, whom she really likes and wants to please, is undermining it all. My first impulse was to call the school and give them a piece of my mind, but Becky begged me not to call. I'm very torn. What about all the girls who don't tell their mothers when they are told to lose weight by teachers and coaches they respect? Do they then internalize the rigid ideals of these misguided mentors? The challenge of counteracting our culture is really more complicated than I thought."

The race to become thin starts early. More than 80 percent of grade-school girls (sixth grade and younger) report having been on a diet at least once. Richard Strauss says in "The Facts" that 40 percent of 9- and 10-year-old girls report having been on a diet, and most of them were not overweight. These feelings of inadequacy leave preadolescent girls with a loss of self-esteem that stays with many of them throughout their adolescence and beyond. Not only do teens feel they must be thin, they also feel pressure to be fit and toned. The problems associated with this lack of self esteem can include thinking and behaviors that become distorted with regard to body image, weight, and diet.

Pretty Poison: Eating Disorders

American culture is preoccupied with body image and weight. For example, according to "The Facts About Figures," the average height and weight of an American girl is 5′4″ and 142 pounds; yet the average height and weight of a model is 5′9″ and 110 pounds. Our advertisements are filled with images of beautiful young women used as backdrops to sell cars, cake mixes, and cell phone service. And while girls are more dissatisfied with their bodies than boys are, boys are not immune to this pressure, either. One of the unintended results of dismantling gender stereotypes is that boys and girls have adopted some of each other's more usual pressures. In addition to their own traditional challenges, like boys, girls are smoking earlier and having sex more indiscriminately. Like girls, boys are paying more attention to their bodies and the desire to conform to a new idealized version of the "buff" young man.

Every girl and mother we spoke with had stories to tell about eating disorders. An excessive struggle for perfection can result in a girl starving herself to attain a dangerous ideal. As a consequence, many girls lead secretive and isolated lives, disconnected from family, friends, and themselves. For example, in "Feminism and Adolescent Girls" Lisa, a sophomore in college, reveals an experience she had with her friend Vanessa.

Lisa said, "From preschool up until fourth grade, I had a classmate named Vanessa. She was friends with everybody, and everyone loved her. Ten years later in Hong Kong, I ran into a mutual friend, Nicki, who was Vanessa's freshman roommate in college. When I inquired about Vanessa, she took out her wallet and showed me a picture of her. Vanessa had the same great smile and the same almost-white blond hair, but then Nicki remarked that she is now anorexic. Later that same summer, I learned that while Vanessa was at Harvard taking a summer course, her anorexia had gotten so bad that she was hospitalized because of it. It made me sad to wonder what happened to the fun-loving, carefree six-year-old that everyone loved?"

The obsession with weight affects more girls than boys; as a result, girls struggle more with eating disorders (see Appendix E: "Warning Signs of an Eating Disorder"). According to one survey, reported in *The Riverdeep Current*, "The Beauty Within," when asked what they would wish for if they had just one wish, the overwhelming majority of girls aged 11 to 17 would wish to be thinner. According to Anorexia Nervosa and Related Eating Disorders, Inc. (ANRED), the focus on weight is particularly painful for girls during puberty, when they gain an average of 40 pounds and grow 10 to 12 inches. Many girls don't understand that weight gained during puberty is not permanent. Puberty is quite a stressful and emotional time, but for these preadolescent girls to be fed a diet of distorted images of women is destructive to their view of what is normal. The American Association of University Women (AAUW) Educational Foundation reported in 1996 that the percentage of American girls who are "happy with the way I am" drops from 60 percent in elementary school to an alarming 29 percent in middle and high school.

While women have achieved much and dismantled many barriers, they still struggle with the weight issue. A London medical school study, reported in "The Beauty Within," reveals that more than half of women overestimate the size of their bodies, when they have no trouble estimating the size of other things. When asked to estimate the width of a box, 50 average-sized women were able to get the width almost exactly. When asked to look in a mirror and estimate the width of their own bodies, the women consistently overestimated the size of their waists by 25 percent and their hips by 16 percent.

It is estimated that 10 million females in the United States— almost all of them teenagers and young women—have serious eating disorders. Although eating disorders, and bulimia and anorexia specifically, are seen most often among more affluent white girls, Ginia Bellafante reports in her January 2003 *New York Times* article, "Young and Chubby," that they also occur among different racial and socioeconomic groups as well as increasingly younger girls. By age 13, 53 percent of girls are unhappy with their bodies; by age 18, 78 percent are dissatisfied.

This is one instance where knowledge may not be a protective factor. In "Creating a Curriculum to Help Girls Battle Eating Disorders" by Sally Giedrys, Catherine Steiner-Adair, director of education and prevention at the Harvard Eating Disorder Center, states, "Teaching about eating disorders can often backfire because it actually can spread the behaviors." In the past, girls would exchange information about vomiting techniques in the school bathroom or at a sleepover; now they can find each other on the Internet anytime.

Websites surface under many names geared to girls who refer to themselves as "Anas," shorthand for anorexics. These sites include photographs of emaciated women that can entice a wavering anorexic back into a destructive eating pattern. Anorexics who would never have communicated with each other before can now find a community of like minds on the Internet. The following two excerpts posted on a website are reported by Joan Ryan in her *San Francisco Chronicle* article, "Overestimating the Fidget Factor": "I refuse to give in to the pathetic whimpers my body makes. I refuse to accept its supposed limitations. I will cross every line it tries to draw. . . . I refuse to let the screams of hunger throw me off" and "Guys, I'm really having a weak moment; I haven't eaten anything at all today, but right now I really, really, REALLY want to. I don't want to give in to the craving, tell me what I should do to forget about it."

Anorexics view eating as weak and are proud of their willpower and control because they are able to endure starvation. The danger in this "outlaw" community is that the aberrant behavior gets reinforced. The support girls give to each other helps them to deny that starvation is dangerous, a denial that ultimately can kill them. Knowledge about the prevalence of eating disorders does not protect our daughters. However, by reducing their perception of the importance of physical appearance, we can mitigate the pressure on them to be excessively thin. We can give our daughters the tools they need to become capable and confident in managing the stress of growing up in our culture of thin. We also need to encourage our girls to exert control over their daily lives in ways other than through food.

Unlike with other issues, mothers and daughters are in this fight together. As one mother of a 17-year-old girl said, "I have been losing and gaining the same 10 pounds since I was 15 years old. Will I ever relax and just accept the size my body really wants to be?" Another mother said, "When I went to a dinner party with a new family I couldn't stop looking at their 14-year-old daughter. Her face was so beautiful, but she was about 20 pounds overweight. I felt bad for her because her mother was so thin and small. I'm so obsessed with my own body size that I find myself ruminating over anybody else's weight." If we express this obsession about weight, our girls will follow our model.

The good news is that some girls and their families can fight back. Seventeen-year-old Robyn said, "My parents always made me feel beautiful. They loved the way I looked. I'm certainly not thin, but I'm not going to allow 10 or 15 pounds [to] stop me from feeling good about myself. I row crew for my high school, and in the boat, my strength and size really matter. Being on the crew team helps me believe that I am much more than my body shape, and if other people have a problem with it, it is their problem, not mine. Look at Queen Latifah; she is definitely a large woman and she sure struts her stuff."

As reported by Ginia Bellafante in "Young and Chubby," Dr. Andrea Marks, a specialist in adolescent medicine, states, "Girls are hearing more messages to take pride in normal body shapes." Several new businesses; a national chain of clothing stores, called Torrid; and Internet companies, such as Alight.com, are targeting the market of teenage girls who want to dress in "hot" clothes like their thinner peers, but in sizes that fit their bodies. Sales are brisk: Torrid has 25 new stores planned for the future, and Alight.com posted a 42 percent increase in sales. These girls don't aspire to be thin, they just want to look cool, according to Bellafante.

Growing Up in Prime Time

Do you find me pretty?
Do I make you laugh?
When my voice cries out are my tears too loud?

These lines from "Do You Find Me Pretty?" a song written by Tracy Carroll, perfectly describe the primary struggles for many adolescents today. The lyrics pose the questions many adolescents ask themselves. Teens wonder, "Am I good enough?" "Am I attractive?" "Am I too vulnerable?" Girls ask themselves these questions for many reasons. Feelings of inadequacy are largely driven by the impossible expectations they get from television and movies. Although female roles have become more varied in recent years, the images remain daunting. With the exception of Camryn Manheim in "The Practice" and China Shavers in "Boston Public" (no longer in primetime), most actors fit the traditional body image stereotypes.

"But also a lot of it's about clothes, and if you're not that skinny, you can't fit into . . . the right clothes that are so in, and I hate wearing tight clothes. When I get home I change."
—Focus group participant

The actors playing the roles of police officers are strong and powerful, but still beautiful and thin; actors playing the roles of lawyers are smart and articulate, but still beautiful and thin; and the doctors are skilled and compassionate, but also beautiful and thin. We continue to give girls a mixed message: as Stephanie said earlier, "A girl can be anything . . . as long as she is thin and pretty." The power of television is so enormous that "70 percent of girls say they have wanted to look like a character on television. About 30 percent have actually changed their appearance or gone on a diet in order to be more like a television character," reports "The Beauty Within."

Too many of our daughters feel invisible or unacceptable. They "are constantly barraged by images of women from a wide array of cultural sources. These sources teach our daughters that power, prestige, wealth, and male attention are the prizes that benefit women who are culturally defined as attractive," report Sharon Mazzerella and Norma Pecora in *Growing Up Girls*. Television teaches girls how to look and how they will be rewarded for being attractive.

Mazzerella and Pecora add that television's impact is huge primarily because it is ubiquitous and children begin absorbing its imagery before they are toddlers. American homes have multiple televisions, DVD players, TiVo, VCRs, computers, and video games. In fact, children aged eight and older spend almost seven hours a day using some form of these machines. Gone are the strict rules of absolutely *no* television in a child's bedroom; 65 percent of kids aged 8 to 18 have a television in their bedroom, according to "The Beauty Within."

Advertisements

Mazzerella and Pecora go on to say that even "television advertising has a powerful effect on young women's body image distortion. Watching as little as a half hour of both advertisements and shows contributes to women's evaluation of their bodies." Ellie, a 17-year-old, said, "I remember looking at the Calvin Klein underwear ads and comparing myself to the bodies in the advertisements. The camera angle gave the models a dramatic elongated look. I'm five feet four inches, and most of my height is from my waist up. I think that I am really supposed to be five feet two inches. The models in the ads were stripped of their clothes and their bodies were so sleek, even the men. Not like mine! I wax, I shave, and I still have bumps. I used to look in the mirror and obsess over my short legs."

It's important to be knowledgeable about what advertisers are trying to sell our kids, how products are packaged, and how the advertisers manipulate consumers using idealized images of men and women. These unrealistic images have a profound power that children internalize, which can be balanced only by acquiring media savvy. The best antidote to the stereotypes perpetuated by the media is to be aware of their power and explain to our daughters that what they are seeing is a distorted reality. We must stress to our daughters that imperfections are real; perfection is not. This knowledge will help to protect them from internalizing stereotypical messages in a negative way.

Magazines: Shop Till You Drop

Ashley, a 17-year-old, said, "It's a little crazy making; these teen magazines try to educate girls about things like birth control and healthy girlfriend/boyfriend relationships, and then they show us looking like tramps in stilettos. I wish they'd make up their minds. Are we adults or kids?" While some of the articles are informative, selling advertisements is what drives magazines. One mother said, "If most girls felt good about themselves, if they didn't smoke, drink, or wear makeup, advertisers would really suffer." Therefore, most teen magazines have resorted to the same ads as women's magazines, featuring rail-thin models and articles about dieting.

In "Trash Mags with Training Wheels," Janelle Brown reports that the teenage market represents $158 billion in spending power and girls spend 75 percent of this money on clothing. Magazines are a perfect vehicle for getting a piece of this pie and heavily influence what teenage girls buy. Girls and boys can benefit from realizing the extent to which they are being targeted as a consumer group and how media messages are used to sell products or services while conveying messages about body image, self-worth, social values, and behavior. One mother said, "My daughter, Devin, knows the names of designers and products I can't afford to buy. She's 16 years old and is saving for a Louis Vuitton purse. Give me a break! I never thought that I'd say this, but at 16 I begged my parents for 13 dollars to buy a pair of Bass Weejuns. Now my daughter is considering spending hundreds, all her allowance and birthday money, on one purse because it makes her feel sophisticated. If she needs a label so badly, I should tattoo one on her wrist."

A good example of the type of shallow messages sent to teens is demonstrated by a feature in a *CosmoGIRL!* magazine that focused on Reese Witherspoon, states "Trash Mags with Training Wheels." Instead of asking her what it's like to be a successful actress, the article focused on "What it's like to be loved by Ryan [Philippe]." The message was who you are and what you do are not as important as who loves you. Once again, a parent's best tool to combat this bombardment of simplistic messages is to help our daughters to attain critical reading and consumer skills.

Look at your daughter's magazines and read them with her. Ask her whether it makes sense that they feature healthy eating while picturing waiflike anorexics selling products. Ask her whether the article about college majors makes sense next to the ad showing the back of a half-naked woman sitting spread-eagle in a very suggestive position.

Explain to your daughter that the photos of the beautiful models are not real, and remind her that those images are the result of the magic of enhanced imagery; with computer software, filters, and touch-ups, we would all look different.

Hope in a Bottle and Barbie, Makeup, and the Dream of Beauty

You also have the power to help shape your daughter's values and ideals. When you label objects to help your daughter understand their function—for example, makeup and Barbie—you can use these tools to demonstrate and teach the character traits you want her to have, such as independence and self-confidence. Any item can function in a positive or negative way; very few objects are intrinsically bad. For example, playing with makeup often functions to assist a young girl's transition from toys to the adult world. Barbie can also serve as a teaching tool.

In her book *Barbie Culture*, Mary Rogers calls Barbie a "fantastic icon" because she expands what is possible and conceivable for little girls—precisely because Barbie is more than her exaggerated figure. Barbie was the first doll that allowed girls to role-play beyond mothering and family, according to Sharon Lamb's *The Secret Lives of Girls: What Good Girls Really Do—Sex Play, Aggression, and Their Guilt.* This expanded play opened up an avenue of exploration to the outside world, including careers and sexuality. Parents can help to determine the meaning of each object for their daughters, and anything can be turned into a teachable moment.

Barbie

We discovered this for ourselves when we discussed the infamous Barbie doll. We learned just as there is no one type of girl, there is also not one right way to raise strong, competent daughters. The following are our personal stories and serve as examples of how parents can use their own values to create lessons and illustrate points they want their daughters to learn. Linda embraced Barbie for personal reasons:

I grew out of Barbie as quickly as I fell in love but was happy to revisit her 16 years later when I gave birth to my very own Barbie fan, my daughter, Emily. With Emily, I made a townhouse out of wood, complete with a milk carton elevator that used a pulley mechanism made from shoelace. We decorated the townhouse with carpet samples and wallpaper remnants and made clothing from fabric scraps and yarn. Barbie's grossly exaggerated proportions make her such fun to dress. She has a spectacular waist, so tiny she could never support her upper torso had she been real, a midsection too narrow for ribs, and rounded mounds without nipples that shoot straight out from her body in perfect form. She always has a stamp on her back, "MATTEL 1958," invariably the perfect reality check that says, remember, I'm not real.

Translated into human dimensions, Barbie's measurements are laughable, and this is more of her appeal. Perhaps, Barbie is a joy for me because she's so politically incorrect. She is my protest against some people's disdain for popular culture. Of course, she's no little girl's role model and no girl's ideal.

But who cares?

Who wants what she has?

Ken, a neatly coifed, synthetic, and pliable man with no genitals; a dream house; a Corvette; or a voice box that once said, "I hate math"?

No, the wonder of Barbie can be experienced in large suburban toy stores. Mounds of pink boxes and the Barbie logo printed in 1950s script create a vast aisle of hot pink.

It's been 45 years, and she's my classic: so bad, she's good. When mothers with no appreciation of trash culture react with surprise or disgust at their daughter's inescapable attraction to Barbie, I relax and think, who cares, give it up, take a trip to Toys "R" Us, and enjoy the ride down the sea of pink.

My feeling was that I would use Barbie to teach certain skills to my daughter and to start a dialogue with her about popular culture. We discussed narrow views of beauty, diversity, career, dating, etc. Because omnipresent popular culture flowed into my house through every electrical outlet, I intentionally permitted my daughter to play with Barbie dolls in an effort to be creative rather than censoring the inescapable messages of popular culture. To use an old real estate phrase, "If you can't fix it, feature it."

A postscript to this is that after all the joking we did about the Barbies that said, "I hate math," Emily overcame that message and took enough science and math to become a physician.

Susan rejected Barbie also for personal reasons:

Barbie was the doll of choice for many of the young girls in the late 1970s and early '80s. I was determined that my daughter, Elizabeth, would have other toys and dolls to play with, not a Barbie. Our living in Berkeley, California, at the time provided her with many other options. She wore coveralls and T-shirts, and pink was not a color in her wardrobe. Even when Elizabeth wore long skirts, as she was prone to do, she would tuck them into her underwear so she could climb to the top of the jungle gym. I knew she played with Barbies at friends' houses, but the values and images in our home served to give Elizabeth an alternate reality. I didn't want her to aspire to look like the blond, blue-eyed, and pink-skinned model whose measurements, if translated into actual human size, would be 5′9″, 39-21-33. With Elizabeth's dark hair, brown eyes, and olive skin, I knew that image was never going to be possible for her.

Barbie perpetuated old myths about what women and girls ought to be. This stereotype represented something quite out of line with the reality of women achieving, performing, and actively participating in American life. I wanted Elizabeth to be at the forefront of social change, not defending old gender-based territory.

Instead, Barbie was released to the world in a revealing bathing suit or high-fashion clothes, ruby red lips, and plucked eyebrows, and she never had a bad hair day. She always had someone to play with and a boyfriend by her side. Barbie had enormous breasts, perfectly fitted clothing, and long legs with painfully arched, perfect feet. Barbie couldn't play sports, if she was even able to walk at all in her stiletto heels. The details of Barbie changed over time, but her body, her whiteness, and her expectations remained the same. Even later on when Mattel created Native American and African-American Barbies, their features remained white. I knew this was not the world Elizabeth would grow up in.

Children and young girls are often uncertain about their self-image. Media, toys, clothes, colors, and so much more can negatively influence them during these vulnerable years. If they don't match up, the effect can be devastating. It isn't only Barbie but the cumulative effect of stereotyping. Barbie didn't create this problem; she is simply a long-standing reminder. As a parent, I could teach Elizabeth what our expectations were for her by not purchasing this kind of doll. She was never deprived as a result of this decision; there were many other toys she could choose from. We would walk through Toys "R" Us and up and down the blinding pink and purple aisles of Barbie and her accessories. We would talk about the meaning of the limited colors, which were thought to be "girl" colors; discuss the way Barbie looked and her limited activities; and talk about how difficult it would be to play, given Barbie's restrictive clothing.

We would compare Barbie to what Elizabeth liked to do and what her hopes and dreams were for her future life. They would include swimming as fast as she could; getting the nickname "Fly," because she was so good at doing the butterfly; piloting airplanes when she was 12 years old; and learning to deal with her dyslexia through persistence and tenacity. Barbie had little to offer in support of these achievements. I think it helped that Elizabeth learned these lessons early in life. She has developed the characteristics necessary to become a strong, self-confident, competent young woman. My anti-Barbie position was one way of supporting her journey to get there.

A phone call from my doctor's office with the results of my amniocentesis in 1983 confirmed my belief that parents are their children's most enduring teachers. At the time, Elizabeth was seven years old. She was standing by my side when the phone rang. After the nurse told us our baby was healthy, she asked whether I wanted to know the sex of the baby. I immediately said, "Yes!" I turned to Elizabeth with the results and said, "Ebeth, you are going to have a baby brother. What do you think?" She thought for a moment and had this serious and determined look on her face, put her hands on her hips, and said, "Well, I'm just going to have to teach him about Title IX!"

We decided to include our personal stories about rejecting or accepting Barbie because they illustrate how you should trust your own instincts to give positive messages to your children. We believe the important ingredients in good parenting are acknowledging your goals and articulating what you value. In our Barbie examples, we used different methods to arrive at the identical objective of empowering our daughters to develop into strong, independent women who could absorb popular culture with a critical eye. In fact, we are not alone. Debra Waterhouse reports in *Like Mother, Like Daughter*, most mothers have a personal reaction to Barbie and "many forbid their daughters from owning or playing with Barbie, while others choose to use this exaggerated twisted ideal as an educational lesson."

Makeup and the Dream of Beauty

In today's culture, makeup serves different purposes for girls of varying ages. Elementary-school girls are first introduced to makeup through play. Many of us worry about our daughters' early interest in makeup and conclude that their attraction to it forecasts obedience to popular culture; others see it differently.

Cathy, the mother of 14-year-old Annie, said, "I'll tell you what I found out with these kids, with my own anyway: they love makeup. They buy makeup a lot, not unlike boys collecting baseball cards or like when I collected Beatles' vinyls. My daughter, Annie, likes to collect makeup and treats it as a cross between a grown-up product and a toy. For Annie and her friends, makeup helps them to straddle both worlds. One of her friends came to our house and I overheard her say, 'Oh, Jennifer, I can talk with you guys later, but I just have to go look at Annie's makeup collection.' It was like saying, 'I just want to see your baseball cards' or something.

"Now, I view Annie's interest in makeup with a whole different mind-set. I realize that the significance that I attach to makeup is too loaded and that it may have a completely different meaning to many preadolescents. I worry that Annie's overly attached to the idea that she has to be a slave to beauty, but I may be overreacting." This mother may be overreacting, but she may not be. With some girls, it is helpful to steer them to a collection that isn't associated with society's mandate to be beautiful. Instead, they could collect something that has to do with their individual interests and passions.

Teenage girls purchase makeup to present themselves to the world in their idealized vision. For older adolescents, makeup no longer exists only in the realm of play. These are the years when girls become worried about how they look and often think about their self-worth and what they believe they can accomplish in terms of whether they feel physically beautiful. Many teenagers see buying and wearing makeup as a passage to maturity and an outward symbol that they are getting older. The problem for girls is when they see their physical appearance as an entrée to social acceptance and believe they will be better liked if they are pretty.

With this in mind, whether or not you condone your teenage daughter's buying and wearing makeup clearly depends on what message she is trying to express. Makeup, in and of itself, is another transitional object, one that can take on a greater or lesser importance. You can make a difference by teaching your daughter how to attach a reasonable significance to its application.

As with all trends, standards for fashion change, while the need to conform to the prevailing standard remains the same. Gone are the pencil eyebrows of the 1940s and thick Brooke Shields eyebrows of the recent past. Nothing remains constant, and teenage girls are taught through TV, movies, advertisements, and magazines exactly what the ever-changing rules are at a given time. How parents cope with these trappings of beauty varies. There isn't one correct way of approaching the use of makeup or any other trend or fashion statement.

PERSONAL BEST

What is "self-image"? Ask your daughter to identify qualities she admires in others. Does she possess those qualities? Is there a large gap between your daughter's self-image and the ideal self-image she described? Is this gap realistic or a creation of unreal expectations?

How would your daughter describe the ideal body for both men and women? Where does the idea of what is an ideal body come from? Is there more importance placed on a woman's conforming to an ideal body than there is for a man? Why? Has the ideal body changed over time? Watch the same television show or movie with your daughter. Discuss each of your perceptions of the main characters in the show/movie. How were the women or girls portrayed? How were the men or boys portrayed? Are they good role models? Do they look like people your daughter knows in real life? Why or why not?

The Sky Is Not Falling: Healthier Messages

Nothing we are saying is news to most of you. You can make a difference in your daughter's acceptance of her body, but it has to begin with a mother's acceptance of herself. You must believe that you are "more than just a pretty face" and be intentional about what messages you send to your daughter.

You should teach your children to be critical consumers by becoming aware of what teenage girls read, listen to, and watch. You can begin by watching and listening to your daughter's programs, reviewing the websites, and talking about them. When teenagers really understand that they are an important consumer group that advertisers target to sell products to by playing on their insecurities, they can become more insightful about what they are reading and seeing. Teens learn that by becoming knowledgeable and critical consumers, they can more successfully resist media pressures.

Positive Trends

Recently, "The Beauty Within" reported that one editor at a teen girls' magazine announced that her magazine would refrain from featuring diet stories and would use more realistic models of all shapes and sizes in the magazine's stories and advertisements. This change came as a result of more aware consumers who spoke out. Other magazines are also beginning to send healthier messages about body image to girls. The cover of the first issue of *Teen Vogue* included "Making It Big: How Curvy Girls Are Changing Hollywood's Stick-Thin Standard." Also, the movie *Real Women Have Curves* featured the main character, played by America Ferrara, advocating for her right to be respected for her larger body. And in one of the most inspiring scenes to appear in recent movies, she undresses and instructs the women working with her to see themselves for the beauties they are, cellulite

WHAT PARENTS CAN DO

* Teach your daughter to become a critical consumer.
* Become knowledgeable about what advertisers are trying to sell your daughter, how the products are packaged to attract her, and how they manipulate consumers using idealized images of men and women.
* Look at your daughter's magazines and read them with her. Explain how she is being targeted as a consumer and that messages from the media, while selling services and products, are also conveying information about body images, self-worth, and appropriate behavior.
* Review websites and programs targeted for your daughter, and discuss them with her.
* Know about retail and Internet companies that sell "cool" clothes in regular sizes.
* Be intentional about what you praise and how you express what is important to you.
* Remember, "the medium is the message." Girls will emulate what they see at home.

and all. We are encouraged by examples that challenge the status quo and expand the notion of what is acceptable. Change happens in incremental steps.

Since Title IX (the federal law that prohibits gender discrimination in education and athletics) was passed by Congress in 1972, we have seen an explosion in the visibility of strong, competent female athletes. Some believe that girls who become more media savvy may reflect the more realistic bodies of superior athletes, such as Serena and Venus Williams. You can use this attitude shift to reinforce the idea that being fit and healthy is beautiful. "Self-Esteem and Young Women" reports that the African-American and Latina influence to the broader culture is helping to redefine the mainstream notion of beauty. Mariela, an 18-year-old Latina, said, "I don't need to see my ribs or feel my bones. In fact, when I'm thin, my face looks sick. Size 12 (on a good day) and size 14 are fine for me. Hey, I'm just a big girl who likes to feel powerful." Mariela speaks for many girls of color who do not feel the same pressure to conform to society's standards of beauty that white girls feel.

Television is beginning to offer girls honest, intelligent, and highly capable role models. Pick almost any prime-time drama, and you now find women portrayed as competent professionals and equal to men. Although still conforming to mainstream standards of beauty, female characters on such shows as "West Wing," "NYPD Blue," "Judging Amy," "Crossing Jordan," "CSI," and "The Practice" are portrayed as skilled professionals. Women in these programs play characters who are confident and independent, no longer the damsels in distress waiting for the prince to save them. In *Reflections of Girls in the Media*, Lois Salisbury reports that television programs, movies, and commercials studied by the advocacy group Children Now show the proportion of women depending on themselves to satisfy their goals to be within a few percentage points of how men are portrayed.

We are aware that the definition of "girls" is slowly changing, as demonstrated by new magazines, fashionable clothes that reflect a real body, and movies such as *Real Women Have Curves*, *Whale Rider*, and *Bend It Like Beckham*, and you should draw on these examples to build resiliency in your girls. If you teach your daughters to be critical observers and consumers, they will learn for themselves the differences between what feels right to them and what doesn't. They will develop confidence in their own opinions, rather than allowing themselves to be overly influenced by what others may think.

Your efforts will enable them to have a broader sense of what is attractive and to put that more accurate vision into perspective. There are more choices for girls in terms of careers, skills, and relationships. We find this to be very encouraging. These are choices girls did not have before. You can use the media as resources to get your messages across. If you have certain values about what is important—achievement, kindness, self-sufficiency, "being sturdy"—you can fight alongside your daughters to resist the barrage of media messages claiming there is only one standard of beauty.

As reported in "The Beauty Within," an international campaign, Turn Beauty Inside Out, now in its third year, focuses attention on how different forms of mass media—movies, television shows, magazines, music videos, etc.—portray girls and women. The goal of this campaign is for industry executives to take responsibility for the images they present and become motivated to create positive messages focused on promoting girls' self-esteem. Creating roles that portray girls and women who are valued for things other than their sex appeal or beauty sends a powerful message to young girls.

You can empower your daughter by teaching her to become a smart consumer and cautious observer of the world around her, including supporting her when she expresses dissatisfaction with what she doesn't like. You can provide guidance by carefully and intentionally choosing what you praise and what you deem to be important. When you praise your daughter's school efforts and athletic abilities, you give her the message that competence and intelligence are what's important. As one mother said, "Looks fade faster than your brain."

The Mirror Has Many Faces

Challenges to Building Competent Spheres

"Like a trapeze artist, the young person in the middle of vigorous motion must let go of [her] safe hold on childhood and reach out for a firm grasp on adulthood, depending for a breathless interval on a relatedness between the past and the future, and on the reliability of those [she] must let go of, and those who will receive [her]."

—ERIK ERIKSON, *Insight and Responsibility*

Modern life offers more choices for young women and girls than at any other time in history. As a result, girls find themselves both confused and exhilarated. Many girls are unaware of the struggles their mothers' generation engaged in to provide this generation with the gains and choices they enjoy. One mother said, "My daughter, Kathleen, can hardly believe that when I played basketball in high school, we weren't allowed to run full court. The coaches must have thought we were delicate weaklings who would pass out if we caught a rebound and ran full court to score. I can remember screeching to a halt at half-court and passing the ball to another player. It seems so antiquated. Kathleen has absolutely no appreciation of how things have changed."

While many of our daughters are more independent than we were at their age, they still struggle to have a positive sense of self. Girls who fare the best both during and after the teenage years develop a secure identity and a flexible set of skills that allow them to address a wide variety of life experiences. As a parent, you can help your daughter by offering sound advice and providing a safe place for her to learn that there is a relationship between her feelings and experiences. If your daughter is feeling rejected by a group of friends, it is appropriate for her to feel sad, embarrassed, and scared. When your daughter is comfortable expressing herself honestly, she validates her feelings and begins to trust what she knows to be true.

We believe that a firm sense of self begins with girls building an internalized set of core values, including these:

* Being accountable for one's behavior; knowing that every action or inaction has consequences
* Understanding that self-acceptance must be valued over social acceptance
* Finding a balance between being true to oneself and responsive to the needs and opinions of others
* Maintaining positive connections with important people in one's life
* Having the courage to honestly articulate one's feelings
* Assuming responsible sexual behavior and engaging in open discussion of sexuality
* Understanding that excessive risk taking can put one's life or health in jeopardy

* Engaging in activities and pursuing careers based on interest and ability rather than gender or the expectations of others

You have tremendous influence on supporting these values, by both what you say and what you do. For girls to internalize these values, you must encourage them to have a voice, enable them to use their voice, and give them the message that what they have to say matters. Preparing yourself to parent and coach your daughter through adolescence takes knowledge about the dynamics of the teenage years and trust in your instincts about what works best for your own child. Adolescence requires a different kind of parenting from raising young children. To be an effective parent, you must move from controlling your child to providing guidance and influence.

Our research and work with focus groups have shown that the most effective way to help your daughter is to assist her in developing an understanding of these core values and how to apply them to her life experiences. Mastery of this process enables her to develop what we call "competent spheres." Competent spheres matter because they provide your daughter with more than one area of proficiency, so that when one sphere fails there is always something else to rely on. In this chapter, we identify the challenges to girls' building competent spheres. In Chapter 9, we provide strategies on how to address them. Challenges include the following:

* Physical changes and brain development
* Having a voice
* Being responsible for her own sexuality
* Tension between being a "nice girl" and being her authentic self
* Pressure to fit in and reliance on external sources for self-definition
* Pressure to be thin and beautiful

* The cult of technology
* Dangers of excessive experimentation
* The frequency of depression in adolescent girls

Responding to these challenges, one parent said to us, "If a girl can have someone she trusts telling her the truth about the options and pitfalls she faces, she feels more confident to face the world."

Let's Get Physical

Eileen, the mother of a 16-year-old, said, "When Sophie enters the room wearing sandals with her three-inch platforms, she towers over me. I'm not used to looking up to speak to her. Her growth spurt seemed to happen overnight. One day Sophie was short, and now I feel like Gulliver's mother. What must it be like to be in that rapidly changing body?" The physical changes in height and sexual development are obvious to everyone; however, the less apparent changes in a teenager's brain are just as dramatic.

With new techniques such as magnetic resonance imaging (MRI), we now understand that the brain overproduces cells and connections, first when we are babies and again during adolescence. At the 2000 White House Conference on Teenagers, Jay N. Giedd, Chief of Brain Imaging at the Child Psychiatry Branch of the National Institute of Mental Health, reported in "Brain Imaging of Children" that the brain is very busy during adolescence pruning and eliminating unneeded connections. According to Daniel Siegel and Mary Hartzell's *Parenting from the Inside Out*, recent research shows that "By adolescence, a process of brain reorganization takes place that shifts the nature of thinking in profound ways." Behavior during the teenage years creates the "hardwiring" for the adult years.

This new information explains why teenagers don't have the same understanding of consequences as adults. Teenage judgment is different. How many times have you asked your daughter with incredulity, "Why did you do that?" and she has answered, "I don't know." "Why did you invite 10 kids to the house knowing that in a millisecond, the situation could explode?" The answer, invariably, is, "I don't know." She gives you this answer because she honestly doesn't know why. Her judgment is affected by the fact that a teenager's brain is not yet fully formed. Specifically, the frontal lobe in the brain, which affects impulse control, is still developing. Therefore, teenagers don't think through consequences as thoroughly as you would.

Because adolescents rely on the area of their brain called the amygdala, they are prone to respond to stimuli with a gut response and are less able to modulate, inhibit, or understand the consequences of their behavior. The amygdala, an almond-shaped area located in the temporal lobe of the brain, is best known for triggering the fight-or-flight response in reaction to fear. Adolescents use the amygdala more to process emotional content, such as fear, until their frontal lobes are developed more fully, when they're in their twenties. The development of the frontal lobe will enable them to be less impulsive and to understand that every action has consequences. Knowing about the science of the brain may not help you to change your child's behavior, but it can help you to better accept and respond to your teenager's angst, her sense of invulnerability, and her attraction to experimentation and risk.

Psychological Theory: Having a Voice

The primary task of adolescence is to build one's identity, which includes social and moral development. Social development explains your daughter's increasing interest in spending time with her peers. During this period, teenagers look to each other for clarification of their values, which helps them individuate (separate) from their family. Much of the classic discussion about adolescence centered around

Erik Erikson's theory of psychological development. According to Erikson, the work of adolescence is "identity vs. identity diffusion," which, in plain talk, means, "Who am I, uniquely?"

Traditional psychological theory defines the stages of boys' growth and development and attempts to fit girls into the same classifications. Until the early 1980s, psychological theory was based exclusively on studies of males. In *The Philosophy of Moral Development*, psychologist Laurence Kohlberg applied Jean Piaget's "preoperational/concrete/formal" distinctions to create a stage theory for the development of moral thinking. However, he built his theory with a narrow view of moral reasoning because he interviewed only male subjects.

Gender is an element of identity that affects an overall sense of self. Stereotypes based on gender can put young women at risk for low self-esteem. As teenage girls worry about how others view them and experience silencing from adults and their peers, they get the message that they shouldn't speak their minds, and girls stop expressing many honest feelings for fear of not being accepted. They may continue to talk a lot, but often they express what they think they ought to say.

In early adolescence, girls begin to lose the ability to trust what they know. Carol Gilligan, a student of Kohlberg's, found that at age nine most girls were able to express their feelings and opinions to family and friends. But by age 12 and 13, many were unable to identify and talk about their feelings and subsumed their "voice," in favor of acting in what is considered appropriate gender-role behavior. In her groundbreaking book *In a Different Voice*, Gilligan explains, "Men think if they know themselves they'll know women. . . . Women think if only they know others, they'll come to know themselves."

When theories are based on men only, women's development may look "abnormal." Gilligan disagreed with Kohlberg's assessment in which he scored women lower or less morally developed than men. She concluded that rather than following rigid rules, women tend to think more about acting in a caring manner, about how their actions affect others. Gilligan determined that women are more likely to consider

"The time between childhood and adulthood is pivotal. The choices teens make, the values they adopt now can determine whether they become happy and productive citizens. Together we can help them to make choices that are good for them, and for all of us."
—HILLARY RODHAM CLINTON, "Parenting a Teen . . ."

their obligations to others in making moral decisions, and men are more likely to consider abstract principles of fairness. She believes that women develop in a way that focuses on connection with others, which includes thinking about oneself and the community (social environment) in which one lives. Their approach to decision making considers their responsibilities to others. Women and men may be different in how they approach problems and solutions, but women's approach is certainly not inferior.

Jenna, a 15-year-old, was asked by her father whether she thought that stealing was wrong. After a few minutes of silence, Jenna responded, "I'm really not sure; it depends on the situation." She added, "If my baby was starving and needed food, I can imagine shoplifting, if I thought that I wasn't hurting the owner of the store." When we think about the context, Jenna's answer becomes a more thoughtful and sophisticated response.

Mental health professionals now question past assumptions in the context of female adolescent development. Many believe that the task of separation and identity must be redefined to address the importance of relationships in the lives of girls and women. Relationships are part of the strength women have and bring into adulthood. Connecting is something most girls and women do well, and this skill serves them in many ways, as long as they don't give themselves away in the process.

Given the importance of relationships in the lives of girls, and based on our research, adolescents don't need to separate from their parents. Rather, teens need to renegotiate their relationship with their parents, while preserving a deep sense of connection. Girls can individuate within the context of a loving family.

When you consider the physical changes of puberty, combined with the rapid development of the brain, psychological challenges for teenage girls are daunting. It's no wonder your daughter vacillates between "Mom, I hate you" and "Mom, you're the best" within the span of an hour. As one father said, "It's a roller-coaster ride, so I fasten my seat belt and brace myself for the ups and downs."

Sexuality: Everything but the Truth

Although teen pregnancy has declined in recent years and there is increased awareness about sexually transmitted diseases (STDs) and use of contraception, girls are participating in sexual activities other than intercourse at increasingly younger ages. Imagine what it's like for girls to come of age at a time of "Sex and the City," when oral sex is the subject of newspapers, when teenage girls are the subjects of pornographic sites, and when underwear is a fashion statement. Everything, it seems, is sexualized.

Because of this early end to our daughters' childhood and the increased sexualization of our culture, girls find themselves in social situations for which they aren't prepared. The "in-your-face" sexuality of today's culture is confusing for young girls. Just think of Samantha on "Sex and the City," who is phobic about intimacy but addicted to sex. Jerry, the father of three teenage girls, said, "No matter what show you turn on, someone is tearing somebody else's clothes off. Sex has become another throwaway."

In the recent past, girls fit into one of two categories: Madonna or whore, angel or temptress, girl next door or slut, clean or dirty. Both sets of categories are fantasies; neither describes a complete person. As Liza Mundy writes in "Sex Sensibility," these categories are "yet another way of sorting girls, setting them at odds with one another. . . . Modern scare tactics have lent a new vocabulary—even a fake veneer of legitimacy—to ancient, pernicious stereotypes." Because of the pejorative characterization of a girl who has sexual feelings, girls learn that finding pleasure in their sexuality is wrong. A boy who is sexually active has status; he's a "player."

Girls and boys should be held to the same standards. Many girls feel forced to have sexual experiences before they are ready. Parents with whom we spoke are afraid for their daughters. It isn't that parents expect their daughters to remain chaste; they just want them to understand that sex is a mature act, to be shared with someone who cares for and respects them.

Whether we like it or not, our daughters are, according to Joan Brumberg's *The Body Project,* "growing up with an expanded repertoire of erotic possibilities." Many girls are becoming as aggressive about sex as boys are. This is a very difficult concept for parents to accept. With different sexual activities, such as oral sex, treated as casual acts, it's no wonder that parents feel out of sync with their teenage daughters. One parent said, "I think my daughter has convinced herself that oral sex is not an intimate act and she can still be a virgin." It appears that girls are engaging in oral sex more frequently to placate boys and alleviate the pressure to do more.

Girls told us that they perform oral sex to satisfy their boyfriends and avoid the possibility of unsafe sex. As with other sexual behavior, a double standard exists with oral sex as well. Many teenage girls mistakenly believe that oral sex is safe sex. This is where dialogue and open communication are so essential. Not talking about sex does not protect your daughter from being sexually active. The converse is true as well: talking about sex does not mean that she will be sexually active. Sex is an uncomfortable topic for parents to deal with, regardless of whether we are liberal or conservative. As a result, we give girls many mixed messages.

Sex is also a less than comfortable topic for our girls. In fact, nearly half of young women recently surveyed by Mary Katherine Hutchinson and Teresa Cooney in *Family Relations* reported feeling somewhat or very uncomfortable discussing sexuality with their parents. However, the same young women reported wishing their mothers and fathers had shared more information with them about sexuality. It makes good sense to discuss sexuality with our daughters. As Brent Miller reports in *Families Matter*, open communication between parents and teenagers has been linked to delaying first intercourse and increasing the likelihood of contraceptive use.

Fathers particularly have difficulty with their daughters' sexuality. Many mothers recounted stories of how differently their husbands perceived the way their daughters dressed. Janice, the mother of 14-year-old Alyssa, said, "This year Alyssa tried a bathing suit on for her dad, and his jaw almost hit the ground. She looked gorgeous. I looked at her wistfully, wishing I could still turn heads like she would. My husband looked at me, puzzled, and said, 'You aren't going to let her go out like that are you?' It was the first time he sounded like a sitcom father. He was really uncomfortable with her sexuality, realizing that she looked sexy and knowing that boys and men might notice." Often, dads more than mothers have a hard time visualizing their daughters being intimate.

As uncomfortable as you may feel, you need to teach your daughter about the duality of sexuality so she can have a safe context in which to explore desire. Girls are taught to keep a rein on the sexual advances of boys, yet they aren't taught how to acknowledge and manage their own sexual feelings. Deborah Tolman says, in *Dilemmas of Desire: Teenage Girls Talk About Sexuality*, that society gives a girl the

"To a generation raised on MTV, AIDS, Britney Spears, Internet porn, Monica Lewinsky, and 'Sex and the City,' oral sex is definitely not sex (it's just 'oral'), and hooking up is definitely not a big deal."
—BENOIT DENIZET-LEWIS, "Friends, Friends with Benefits, and the Benefits of the Local Mall"

unfair choice between connection with herself and her body, including sexual feelings, and denying her body pleasure.

Today's parents came of age at a time when they worried that unprotected sex would lead to pregnancy. Our daughters have come of age in a world where sex can lead to AIDS and death. Ellen, the mother of three teenage daughters, said, "When I was a teenager, my fear about being sexual was focused on worrying if I'd ruin my reputation as a 'nice girl' or get pregnant. Now I teach my daughters about date rape and disease. Since the late 1970s sex can kill you, and I worry whether my daughters will be casual about protecting themselves." Ellen is right; acronyms that we never heard of—STDs, HIV, and AIDS—are now in our vocabulary, and the adolescent community is not as knowledgeable as it needs to be about these risks if young people are to be safe.

Parents worry that when their daughters acknowledge their sexual desires, the girls will be more vulnerable to danger. In contrast, when girls begin to trust their own minds and bodies, they gain a stronger sense of self, which will help them to make safer decisions. In addition, Liza Mundy claims in her article in the *Washington Post* that teens "who have a strong, healthy relationship with at least one parent, where they can talk about what's on their mind and what they're dealing with are less likely to have early sexual experiences." To be able to identify their sexual feelings and to listen to their bodies are significant responsibilities girls must undertake as they mature.

Slutty Dressing

Today's fashions are more physically revealing than ever before, and parents are battling with their daughters about what is too sexual. Many mothers reported that they would have died if their slip showed when they were girls. What girls even wear slips today? Underwear is now outerwear. Girls are dressing more and more provocatively and at younger ages, succumbing to the manipulation of mass media and culture. Slutty dressing can be viewed in two very contradictory ways.

On the one hand, you can see revealing dressing as a statement of independence and freedom. On the other, slutty dressing is capitulation to gain attention through self-debasement.

Ellen, the mother of 13-year-old Lucy, said, "I am mortified to admit that last week, I told Lucy she looked like a slut. I know that calling your child names is found in the 'don't ever do that' section of any child-rearing manual, but I finally lost it. She wears her pants below her navel and layers two tank tops with her bra straps hanging out. When did Cyndi Lauper become a style maven? I'm at a loss. All her friends, some of them really good students, dress incredibly provocatively, so I'm confused about how much to rein her in. I don't think she understands what message she is sending to boys and men. I'm worried that someone will take advantage of her." Ellen's concerns are validated by our conversations with young men. In talking with young men aged 22 to 30, we learned that they are uncomfortable with this "in-your-face" sexuality of young girls. Many were concerned because they could no longer distinguish between girls they could ask out and "jailbait."

In response to the greater cultural reality of how clothing is sold to girls, parents should educate their daughters about how to avoid being used as objects to market clothing and line the pockets of corporations. Too often, parents are reluctant to step in and assert their authority because they want their daughters to "fit in." You need to make sure that your daughter, in the name of self-expression, is not projecting an unintended message—one more sexual then either she or you believe she intended.

Sugar and Spice and Everything Nice . . .

Boys start to hide their vulnerability and mask their feelings at the age of four or five. Girls start to hide their (controversial, messy) feelings and lose trust in what they know at age 12 or 13. This happens because of the enormous pressure they feel to be "nice girls." Our culture expects girls to be sensitive, caring, and nice, which "creates a burden on girls that plays into a larger myth that 'girls are good.' The 'tyranny of the nice and kind,' a phrase coined by Lyn Mikel Brown and Carol Gilligan, forces girls to express in public those aspects of girlhood that people expect," as Sharon Lamb reports in *The Secret Lives of Girls*. This loss of voice is often experienced as a sacrifice necessary for connection, because for them to stay in relationships with other girls, they may have to avoid the truth of their own experience. As a consequence, girls' ability to speak truthfully and trust what they know goes underground.

After speaking with girls, Carol Gilligan discovered that what psychologists had assumed was human nature regarding the development of adolescent girls was, instead, "an adaptation to a particular human landscape." Gilligan notes that the girls vacillated rapidly between knowing and not knowing, which she describes as a "cover story and an under-reality." She interviewed one girl who said, "If I were to say what I was feeling and thinking, no one would want to be with me, my voice would be too loud." On the surface, silencing may seem contradictory to girls talking a lot, but they frequently spend their time presenting a "cover story," rather than expressing their real feelings. You will need to make sense of the chatter and guide your daughter skillfully toward saying what is really on her mind.

According to Lyn Mikel Brown and Carol Gilligan in *Meeting at the Crossroads: Women's Psychology and Girls' Development*, the images of "the perfect girl" and "the nice girl" create a burden for girls as young as 10. During this period, according to researchers, many middle-class teens internalize the messages and expectations that the "perfect girl" is pretty, polite, compliant, and free from contrary or independent feelings and thoughts. Holly, a ninth grader in a large public high school, said, "I think I'm controlling because whenever I'm part of a group project, I take charge. It just feels natural to start organizing and get to work. I try not to be bossy, and whenever anyone complains I immediately step back and listen to their ideas about how to proceed. My mother says that I'm not controlling and if I were a boy I would be considered a leader." In surveying teachers in *Failing at Fairness: How America's Schools Cheat Girls*, Myra Sadker and David Sadker found that a teacher's least favorite student is a noncompliant girl—who runs counter to traditional gender expectations.

Holly is fortunate, because her parents point out that society has a double standard for boys' and girls' behavior. This awareness enables Holly to reframe her "controlling" identity into the identity of a leader. We believe that when girls try to keep up with the impossible demands of this unrealistic view of "perfect" feminine behavior, they must suppress some of their ability to express anger or to assert themselves. The pressure to conform causes girls to view themselves through the eyes of others, which prevents them from accurately judging their sense of self-worth.

Fitting In

In addition to the tyranny of beauty and niceness, there are other standards of perfection teens are compelled to meet. Teenage girls are obsessed not only with how they look but also with whether they belong to the right crowd and how popular they are with boys. Overemphasis on fitting in fosters a disregard for uniqueness and individuality. The pressure to fit in, to achieve in school, and to be nonthreatening to boys and other girls can chip away at a girl's self-image. Consumed with being liked by others, she doesn't get around to liking herself.

As Susan, Hillary's mother, said, "Hillary is reserved and anxious to please. She wants to be liked more than anything else. She is so self-effacing that she doesn't take credit for what she does and is much more comfortable in the background. I know this because I watch her stepping back and waiting to hear how her friends think before she speaks. Sometimes I overhear her agreeing with her friends about something that we've talked about, and I know she really has a different opinion."

In general, teenage girls are continually stuck in the cycle of wanting to be unique *and* accepted all at the same time.

Julie, 16 years old, said, "On Monday, I had five girlfriends who ate lunch with me every day at the same table in the cafeteria. On Tuesday, I felt an icy chill when I put my tray of food down at the table. Natalie looked up from her sandwich and snarled, 'Julie, there's really no room here for you!' I was totally clueless about what was going on, and I practically had to get on my knees to find out why Natalie was mad. I apologized for something I don't even think I did, but it was the easiest way to avoid her anger. I was scared that she'd get my other friends to treat me like a leper. What really gets me is that I never call her on how petty she is. I'm too chicken to shake the boat, so I suck it up and hold it in."

In these instances, Hillary and Julie, like so many other girls, have chosen to be silent and hide their real opinions to avoid conflict. They have learned that hiding part of themselves is a way to maintain their place in their groups. Girls' friendships in adolescence are filled with pitfalls because their social life involves negotiating cliques, gossip, and power plays. Gossip is the noise that girls accept within their peer groups and allows them to express unsafe feelings, such as anger and aggression, which are not permitted in a more direct way.

Nothing can protect your daughter from rejection and the worry about whether she fits in. To protect herself, your daughter must be able to create, maintain, and communicate her personal boundaries to other girls. If she can hold onto the knowledge that she is ultimately "OK" in the face of power plays and feeling rejected, then the pain of unkind words will lose some of their power and she'll feel more self-confident.

Low self-worth contributes to a more general dissatisfaction, which can set a teenage girl up for free fall. Besides a decline in academic performance, researchers such as Elizabeth Debold, writing in *Principal,* have found that "Compared to boys, adolescent girls experience greater stress, are twice as likely to be depressed, and attempt suicide four or five times as often (although boys are more likely to be successful)."

Being accepted is the holy grail for teenage girls, who put enormous value on fitting in. Society has taught women to become so focused on their imperfections that they fail to see what is unique about themselves. Girls want to be popular because being so mitigates their imperfections. Popularity depends on fitting in, which includes dressing just right and conforming to the rules of the group. This desire is so strong that many are willing to go under the knife to enhance what they didn't get naturally, deny their hunger, and lose touch with themselves.

You are better able to cut through the noise when you are able to identify the challenges in your daughter's life. This knowledge gives you an entry into many conversations that you can use to help your daughter sort through and make sense of her feelings in order for her to make good choices. This process will allow your daughter to begin to know and appreciate who she is, identify what she stands for, determine what her values are, and set boundaries that can better protect her from unhealthy and risky behaviors. Your daughter's tales and endless information may distract you, but this period requires looking beyond the actual words to fully comprehend the reality of her experience.

Girls are influenced and formed by the strong messages they receive from parents, culture, their peers, and schools. Girls need to disconnect from cultural pressures that require them to subjugate their self-esteem and their voice to the group (peers and/or culture). They should be encouraged to find and speak their own truth.

Popularity: Invitation for Trouble

As reported by AAUW in *Gender Gaps—Where Schools Still Fail Our Children*, girls in grades six and seven rate being popular and well liked as more important than being perceived as competent or independent. Boys, on the other hand, are more likely to rank independence and competence as more important. Take 14-year-old Michelle, who reports, "Sometimes I act like I'm not as intelligent as I really am. I feel that if guys knew that I have a four-point average, they would be intimidated—I have found this to be true." In mathematics courses, for example, girls start attributing their good grades to luck rather than skill. Girls need our support and the support of other adults to resist pressures to conform to outdated stereotypes that limit their expectations and achievement in favor of popularity, just like the character portrayed by Lindsay Lohan in *Mean Girls*, when she denied her ability in math to get the boy.

The impact of the need for popularity can damage a girl's self-esteem. In a 2002 study by the Carnegie Council on Adolescent Development, only 39 percent of high school girls were reported to have high self-esteem levels, compared to 55 percent of high school boys. As a parent, you contribute to this pressure when you are overly invested in your daughter's popularity. If you are, you reinforce the message that her value is measured by her social status and how others view her. For example, while there's nothing wrong with telling our daughters they are lovely, it can suck the life out of them when we pay too much attention to their appearance.

Girls are now exhibiting eating disorders as young as age 11, and more and more teens are turning to cosmetic surgery such as breast implants and rhinoplasty to find that perfect look to satisfy their belief that it will make them more popular. As one teen admitted, "I believe being thin would solve all my problems." Over and over we heard girls say, "The pretty girls are the popular girls." Research reports that the most important goal for most women is to lose 10 or 15 pounds. For too many, this goal translates into cosmetic surgery or disordered eating.

As Naomi Wolf concludes in her book *The Beauty Myth*, the aspect of the beauty myth's manipulation of mass culture that is most stifling for women is that they are both the perpetrators and the victims of their own oppression. In a world where every woman must struggle with issues regarding her body image, the plight of the beautiful and the plight of the plain are strikingly similar. This perspective is supported in an article titled, "Angry Girls Use Friendship as a

Weapon," by Joanne Kates, who writes, "I was never popular. Saturday nights in high school, I was the one with nothing to do. . . ." She added that one of the very popular girls from her high school moved across the street from her 25 years later, and when they reunited, she said, "You were popular," and the woman replied, "I never thought so, I thought you were."

After this encounter, Kates writes, "Even the girls who are perceived as winners sometimes see themselves as losers, and it's no better today than when I was a teenager." As an adult, Kates finally realized that whether you are plain or pretty, popular or not, there are things about yourself you don't like. Everyone struggles and deals with uncertainties and insecurities, and, often, girls only think someone else has it better. But your daughter won't know that until she is older, just as most of us didn't know it.

We must understand and acknowledge that our daughters live in a world that defines them by how desirable they are as women. Popularity demonstrates to our daughters that they are wanted and, therefore, more desirable as both friends and girlfriends. It is better to help girls figure out how to cope with the pressure—to know where to make compromises and understand where not to make compromises. Learning to function in our culture is the first lesson in the exercise of girl power. We can help our daughters by discussing our own ambivalence regarding cultural expectations. When you express your honest feelings about how you are also affected by the enormous value our culture places on popularity and being desired, you build credibility with your daughter.

Beauty: What if You Have a Daughter Who Doesn't Look Like Hilary Duff?

We baby boomers have questioned everything, except, for the most part, the standards and ideals of beauty and body image. If the amount of money and/or time spent on makeup, cosmetic surgery, and skin care products is any indication, we are still trying to meet these unrealistic ideals. We try to look young at any cost. In fact, CNN.com reported that from 1997 to 2001 there was a 304 percent increase in the number of cosmetic procedures. Therefore, it should come as no surprise that our daughters have taken in these messages. We are teaching our daughters to sculpt their bodies, appearance, and behavior into what others expect.

We can't overemphasize how important it is to be aware of the messages you give your daughter about her appearance and her weight. Depression in girls is often connected to negative feelings about their physical features and appearance. Popular culture encourages gender stereotypes in television, magazines, movies, and fashion industries that present challenges to girls' healthy psychological development. The issue of body image is challenging for parents and their daughters. Lydia, the mother of 17-year-old Samantha, said, "It was pure heartache when I took my daughter, Samantha, to get a prom dress for the junior prom. She cried and said that every dress made her look fat. After looking at the pile of crumpled gowns on the dressing room floor, I felt so disappointed, frustrated, and sad that her image was so distorted. I finally said to her, 'Samantha, how could you look fat in a size 8?' I haven't been a size 8 since I was in seventh grade. Get real; don't ruin a potentially wonderful time with an inaccurate self-perception!"

A teenage girl's constant worry about how the outside world views her is distracting. These worries drain a girl's energy, enthusiasm, and focus on other things. The energy that girls use to hyperfocus on their popularity, beauty, and fitting in could better be used to play sports, study, and pursue hobbies.

While much of the pressure to be thin comes from the media, the earliest and most influential messages regarding your daughter's body come from you. Your unintended comments can make the difference in whether your daughter can resist this pressure. The easiest way for you to encourage your daughter's healthier body image is to refrain from commenting about being chubby or having baby fat. It is perfectly normal, for example, for young adolescent girls to have body fat. Most young girls put on weight before they enter puberty and grow; this is nature's way of getting women ready for reproductive development.

Teenage pudginess was more accepted in the past. JoAnn Deak, author of *Girls Will Be Girls*, states, "When most of us were this age, prepubescent girls weren't expected to look like glamour models." Beauty doesn't guarantee self-esteem. Physical appearance is only one factor; it may get you in the door, but it doesn't keep you there. We need to give these types of messages to our daughters. But sometimes we can learn these lessons from our daughters.

Alison, an 18-year-old high school senior, told us about her mother's fixation on her body. Alison said, "Ever since I can remember, my mother warned me about getting fat. I was never fat but could always stand to lose about five to ten pounds. I know that this doesn't sound like much, but all of it sits on my hips and rear, and I can go down a whole pants size if I lose the weight. My closet has two pants sizes: chubby Alison and thin Alison. I am not as tortured by this as my mom. Even when I feel fine about myself, I sense her eyes settling on my rear. She offers me unwanted advice on how to dress defensively and looks pretty outraged when I don't try to mask my figure faults. When I ask her why she just won't give it up, she tells me that it's for my own good.

"Thank God for sports. It's been like an antidote to my mom's pressure for me to be thin. I think I have a healthier view of my body because I'm athletic and play varsity field hockey. These legs work fine. My hips and rear don't interfere with my performance on the field, and most guys don't seem to mind either." Alison's story is a good example of the protective function of having other spheres of interest in one's life to increase opportunities for developing a positive self-concept. Girls who are athletic present themselves with confidence for many reasons. They are fit and tend to have higher self-esteem. Athletic girls are busy with another interest that is about their performance, not about their appearance, and they have an opportunity to create deep bonds of friendship that can develop between teammates.

IM: The Unspoken Word

"Sesame Street" and its rapidly changing images were just a tiny glimpse of what the future held for our children. Transitions now happen for children so quickly that haste has taken the place of introspection and careful analysis. E-mail has replaced letter writing, and instant messages (IMs) are fast becoming as important as the telephone to connect teenagers to one another. IMing and cell phones have created a world of unfiltered instant communication.

According to Ellen Edwards's May 2003 article, "Middle Schoolers, Letting Their Fingers Do the Talking," America Online "estimates that by 2005, IMs will surpass e-mail as the primary way of communicating online. Right now 1.6 billion AOL and IMs are sent every day." The Internet and instant communication create a new landscape for teenage interaction, and their full impact is not yet known. So far, what we see as challenges are the lack of filtering messages, the ability to send these messages to people not of your own choosing, and your daughter's access to inappropriate and unwanted information.

This instant communication can be a risk to friendships because it increases the speed of gossip and offers a quicker way to gang up. Girls told us numerous stories of going to school and discovering that last night's private message was today's general knowledge. Girls who were your friends yesterday no longer spoke to you.

In the past 10 years, parents have been unable to make their home a space where their children are sheltered from the "more adult real

---

"I've gotten into a billion fights because of IMing, when the person reading it misunderstood my message. Now I just use e-mail. I feel I have more control."

—Focus group participant

world." New dangers exist because parents can no longer control with whom their daughters connect via the Internet, who can contact them, or what images they see. One father said, "I knew how sketchy the Internet can be after I discovered that my own well-adjusted 14-year-old son joined chat rooms claiming to be a 23-year-old woman. How does anyone know who they are talking to?"

Another mother said, "On one new Internet site, unsolicited pornographic photos open up without my double clicking. I find it offensive and intrusive. I also get several e-mails per day selling me penis enlargements. Who knew there was a market for such a thing?" With the recent advent of virtual communities, Internet, e-mail, instant messaging, and chat rooms, we have little control over whom our children communicate with. Teens are being exposed to values and information without the benefit of parental supervision or analysis. Therefore, you have to help your kids be more savvy because some real street dangers can now enter your kitchens, living rooms, and bedrooms through the Internet.

Experimentation and Risky Business

Today, our children live in more dangerous times and with a higher state of anxiety than we did as teens. Studies also show that smoking is on the rise among young women. Girls as young as 12 are smoking. What is interesting in terms of gender differences is that boys begin smoking because of the influence of their peer group, but girls are more likely to smoke if their parents do. Marijuana is more potent now than ever before, date rape drugs are readily available, and sexual activity with unknown partners can be lethal.

The U.S. Department of Education reports on its website that 15 million kids go home to an empty house every day, one-half of them under the age of 14, setting the stage for risk taking and exploration without adult supervision. Risk taking is both normal and developmentally appropriate during adolescence. Teens take risks to see for themselves what works and what doesn't, to find out who they are and who they aren't, to test limits, and to create a unique sense of themselves. However, some of what they experiment with can be dangerous, especially today. The following scenario describes how risk creeps into a normal social activity:

Your teenage daughter goes to a party with kids she knows, so she thinks she has no reason to be afraid. Someone secretly drops a drug like Rohypnol or Ecstasy into her drink. When the drug dissolves, it is colorless and odorless. As she consumes the drug, it takes effect. Under the influence of either one of these drugs, she may experience drowsiness, dizziness, confusion, lack of coordination, loss of inhibition, impaired judgment, and reduced levels of consciousness. We all shudder when we think about what can happen under these circumstances.

This is a cold and scary scenario. Some parents ignore this reality, while others are consumed with anxiety about the dangers that can befall their daughter. Knowing this type of risk exists requires you to present this information to your daughter in a way that strikes a balance between scaring the daylights out of her and teaching her to be alert to and aware of her environment.

Girls can have a good time, grow up, and test limits. We have to acknowledge that experimentation is a normal part of development. Yet, if you suspect that your child is excessively using drugs and alcohol, then, of course, you need to step in. Knowledge is power, and to gauge how your daughter is handling her life, you have to be aware of what's out there.

Susan, the mother of Nikki, said, "During my daughter's teenage years, I always had a clear understanding that my role was to find a balance between letting my daughter go to parties where she might be faced with temptations and keeping her out of harm. The challenge for me was knowing how to find that balance. Some of the other mothers of my daughter's friends were clueless and still believed that they could keep their daughters safe at parties by making sure that a parent was home. I learned how naive this was pretty early in Nikki's life, the day after I let her attend a class sleepover on the last day of third grade (this was an all-girls' school).

"The morning of the party, Nikki woke up with her first migraine after not sleeping at all the night before. She told me that the girls played outside after midnight, and many of them stayed up all night. The host's parents, seemingly responsible, with a house big enough to hold the entire class, spent the night in their bedroom, while the girls had a 12-hour free-for-all. This was my rude awakening. I knew that after this early experience, the presence of parents did not necessarily offer my daughter any real protection. They probably had strict orders from their daughter to be invisible."

Another father told us how his daughter cried and pleaded with him not to call the boy's parents at the home of a party. He said, "Through her sobs, she cried, 'Dad I'll die if you call; no one's parents call; it will be the kiss of death. I won't go, just don't call!' And she's right. I've asked around; after a while most parents stop calling."

Many parents had personal stories that rivaled the plot of the movie *Risky Business*. One mother said, "Your house is a bull's-eye if you aren't home. Imagine how fast the news of your absence spreads with cell phones and e-mail. My daughter, Rachel, invited a few of her friends to our house when my husband and I were going to be away for the weekend (the first time in seven years). Rachel, in her naiveté, thought she could put up tape to block off the newly decorated living room, believing that a masking tape barrier would protect my new furniture from 200 of her 'closest' friends.

"We decided to go away because of our friends' willingness to house-sit. They parked their car in front of the house in order to prevent kids, who came in droves, from entering the house. Our friends observed a *Field of Dreams*–like line of car headlights for the entire block and around the corner. My daughter knew that there were going to be more kids than she had planned when groups of kids from other high schools descended on the house."

Many other parents had similar stories. Donna, Stephanie's mother, said, "During Steph's first high school party, she had the largest boy, a defense tackle, guard the food while the jewelry upstairs was left unguarded. Did she think the milk and American cheese were more valuable than my engagement ring?" That's how naive they are. Their judgment is that of a teenager, and consequences seem less important than the attraction of doing something they know they aren't supposed to do. No matter how smart your daughter is, you can't anticipate how convoluted her reasoning can become. As we discussed earlier in this chapter, your daughter's judgment and ability to forecast consequences are not fully developed.

As a parent, you must protect your child and yourself from the potential consequences of these incidents, knowing how out of hand they can get in a flash. These years take a kind of parental vigilance the military would be proud of. Those of you who have tried to substitute an older sibling for an adult find it does not work very effectively because that sibling is stuck between a rock and a hard place; he or she has to straddle two roles. This is a time of life when no one really should substitute for an attentive parent or other caring adult.

Experimentation, which is a normal part of adolescent exploration, often includes alcohol and drugs. However, there is a major difference between teenage exploration and the use of alcohol and drugs for self-medication. If your daughter suffers from depression, struggles with other psychological diagnoses, such as bipolar disorder, or has been the victim of abuse, she may use drugs and/or alcohol to self-soothe.

Drinking and Drugs

The Substance Abuse and Mental Health Services Administration (SAMHSA) reports in "Alcohol Use Among Girls" that depression and substance abuse often occur together. It is often not clear which comes first: depression leading to use of alcohol or drugs to alleviate the symptoms, or use of drugs and alcohol leading to depression. Recent studies conducted by the National Center on Addiction and Substance Abuse at Columbia University found that approximately 45 percent of high school girls drink alcohol, compared with 49 percent of boys; girls use prescription drugs more than boys do; and the number of girls who start drinking between the ages of 10 and 14 has risen from 7 percent in the 1960s to 30 percent in the 1990s. Friends and peer pressure also particularly influence girls when it comes to drinking and taking drugs. They want to fit in, even if doing so is dangerous.

It's hard for today's teens to escape the alcohol industry's media bombardment and to resist peer pressure to drink. While some parents experience relief that their teen is "only" drinking, rather than taking drugs, they may not recognize the fact that alcohol *is* a drug. Teens use alcohol more frequently and heavily than all other illicit drugs combined, according to a 2000 National Institute on Alcohol Abuse and Alcoholism publication, *Make a Difference: Talk to Your Child About Alcohol*. Alcohol kills 6.5 times more teens than all other illicit drugs combined, and this does not take into consideration the countless life-altering consequences of underage drinking that do not result in death. According to the "National Household Survey on Drug Abuse Main Findings 1997," girls participate in binge drinking more frequently than in the past, having caught up with boys. We don't think encouraging more independent behavior for girls means taking on the dangerous, risky behaviors previously dominated by boys.

According to "A Parent's Guide on Teenagers and Drinking," 11 million underage young people drink each year, and 12 is the average age when a child takes his or her first drink. Judy, the mother of Jacob, said, "At Jake's 12th birthday party I had a rude awakening. About eight boys and girls sat around my kitchen table pretending to chug down beer, using salad dressing. I had only been out of the kitchen for 15 minutes when I realized that they were playing drinking games." Again, this is not so surprising in light of the statistic that 30 percent of kids admit to binge drinking in high school.

It's important that you talk to your daughter about the dangers of combining drinking and sex. The most dangerous thing for a girl to do is to drink with a boy she doesn't know well. Blair, an 18-year-old college freshman, told us that she thinks she was date raped after a fraternity party. She said, "How horrible is it to not even know if I was violated? It haunts me, and I'm not sure what to do. I wasn't conscious enough to trust what I really think went on. I want to confront him, but I'm not sure exactly what happened. I remember passing out while lying on this boy's bed. We were messing around, and I woke up a few hours later half-dressed. I don't know whether to be humiliated or outraged." Blair's experience is too familiar. The National Council on Alcoholism and Drug Dependence states that two-thirds of sexual assaults against female teens and college students take place when they and/or others are drinking.

Alcohol can cause a group situation to get particularly out of hand. In 2003, teenage girls pounded each other during a touch football game that degenerated into a muddy brawl. Five girls were injured in a violent free-for-all that involved 100 students. After this hazing incident at Northbrook High School in Illinois, Kathleen Parker reported in "What Are Little Girls Made Of? How About Pig Guts and Beer?": "Girls will be girls. Give them a couple of kegs, some pig intestines, and a bucket of human feces and, well, stuff happens. . . . But rules have a funny way of getting broken, especially when alcohol is present and parents are missing. The powder puff ritual was held in a 'secret' place and was lubricated with a couple of kegs of beer that police say may have been procured by parents. One parent also may have helped collect the feces, according to early reports." The parents who provided the alcohol for this daytime activity were charged with furnishing alcohol to minors.

Teenagers push the limits. It is normal for them to experiment and take risks to grow up and develop. According to Dr. Michael Riera in his appearance on "Oprah" on March 26, 2003, "You can say anything you want, if your kid is going to have any kind of social life . . . they are going to experiment and be in social situations that involve underage drinking."

You are still responsible for setting limits, however. We know teens fight these limits, but they do need and even want them. Limits help to contain them while they are experimenting and still developing. Limits communicate to your daughter that, while you may act like a friend, you are still very much a parent. One parent talked about participating in a parent peer group while her daughter was in high school. Issues such as curfews, driving, and drinking were discussed. Two of the parents in the group, Sara and Rob, looked at the rest of the group with condescension. They didn't understand what the concern was because they thought that discussing these issues meant the others couldn't control their own children. Sara said, "I don't know what your problems are, but my son and daughter are in every Friday and Saturday night before midnight."

The rest of the group hid their disbelief at the naiveté of these parents. They knew that virtually every Friday night those kids were sneaking out of the house, and one father in the group had caught their daughter smoking pot in his kitchen. One of the parents in the group gently told Sara and Rob about the reality of their children's behavior. They discussed together how they could communicate better with their own kids and gave them a sense of reality, along with what their expectations should be.

Sara and Rob decided to extend their kids' curfew with the understanding that they were going to create an environment for more honest and open communication. They also reiterated their messages and values to their children regarding alcohol and other drugs. Many teenagers we spoke with said their parents often didn't set clear rules about alcohol and other drugs. If parents don't condemn drinking, even when they know it's going on, they force kids to set their own limits.

The teenagers with whom we spoke also said they aren't disciplined routinely when they break the rules. It's tough to sort through all the mixed messages that society promotes about alcohol, which is why your child deserves a clear, consistent message from you and consequences when rules are broken, such as taking away the car keys or grounding them. Consequences that match the offense and are given in real time are most effective.

Depression

During childhood, girls and boys experience depression with equal frequency. In adolescence, however, according to Leah Carlson in "Five Middle Schools Launch Program to Deal with Depression," girls are twice as likely as boys to experience depression. The University of Michigan Depression Center's website reports in "Understanding Depression" that adolescent girls may be predisposed to depression because of the "increase in hormones associated with puberty, changes in body shape and emerging sexual identity, family stressors such as divorce and peer pressure."

Many parents find it hard to distinguish a daughter's real sadness from the drama and moods of teenage life. However, this is one time when it is crucial for you to be able to make sense out of all the noise. Girls have a hard time expressing their sometimes dark and complicated feelings, because they learn that expressing their honest feelings can be dangerous. Girls come to understand they shouldn't share intimate feelings that can be used against them or disagree or fight in a confrontational way for fear of being shunned. By the age of eight, young girls are sensitive to being whispered about by other eight-year-old girls. Telling secrets and whispering teach girls that it's too dangerous to call attention to strong feelings.

Girls express their power in relationships with indirect forms of aggression. Because girls are prohibited from expressing their anger in direct ways, they learn to be covert or to suppress their anger. Suppressed anger does not get digested, and it can become self-destructive, manifesting itself in depression and self-mutilation—bingeing, purging, and cutting. If girls can't be their authentic selves, they are more vulnerable and likely to turn their sadness inward.

Sometimes it is difficult to tell what is normal adolescent angst and what is real depression. This is where your instincts are critical. You are the best judge of your daughter because you know her sleeping and eating habits and favorite activities. Symptoms of depression include changes in these activities. Any sadness that persists for more than two weeks should be a cause for concern (see Appendix D for symptoms of depression).

Suicide, which has increased dramatically among teens in recent years, is the third leading cause of death for 15- to 24-year-olds and the sixth leading cause of death for 5- to 14-year-olds, according to "Teen Suicide." Girls attempt suicide more often than boys do, but because they have learned (at least better than boys) how to ask for help, they are less successful at ending their lives. This is an extreme and drastic measure to manage their pain. Girls also tend to use less aggressive ways to attempt suicide. But, regardless of the method, parents and those who work with teens must take their verbal and nonverbal cues seriously to try to prevent a tragedy from taking place.

Cutting

The subject of cutting is extremely upsetting, and most parents don't know how to approach it. As with anorexia and bulimia, girls teach other girls how to cut themselves. The tendency to mimic the behavior of others at this age is compelling, and sometimes what is first an experiment becomes a compulsion that is hard to give up. Through self-mutilation, girls communicate that they are hurt and are unable to put their pain into words. The carving into flesh and watching the bleeding is an avenue of release from their mental pain. In our focus groups, girls told us that sometimes when they are feeling emotionally

"As her grades slipped, she withdrew from family and friends. Angry and profoundly frustrated, the 12-year-old bought a 10-pack of razor blades. Over the course of the next year, she slashed her wrists without causing serious injury at least 15 times—whenever she scored badly in a test or had a fight with friends. 'It almost became a stress relief for me . . . an emotional letting-go.' "
—SUSAN HORSBURGH and JOANNE FOWLER,
"A Survivor's Tale: Bouncing Back from Despair"

numb, experiencing physical pain helps them to know that they are alive and real. Cutting is a sign that you need to intercede immediately and help your daughter learn healthier ways to identify and cope with her painful feelings.

If you suspect your daughter is engaging in this behavior, it is important to seek professional help. Therapy can help her to identify the areas of her life over which she feels she has no control and to gain insight into the emotions she isn't able to access on her own. While insight isn't a panacea, it is your best weapon against your daughter's destructive behavior. Insight sets our daughters on the path to understanding what they need to help themselves. Only when they know what they need can they begin to meet those needs.

Improving the "Days of Our Lives"

The challenges to girls developing a variety of strengths and interests (competent spheres) that they become proficient at are many. The images of women in the media and the pressure to fit in, to achieve in school, and to be nonthreatening can chip away at a girl's self-esteem.

Experimentation rightfully makes parents anxious, but you have to be realistic about what is going on and work with your daughter to cope with risks. You are better able to cut through the noise when you can identify the challenges in your daughter's life. Putting your head in the sand and maintaining a belief that other daughters—but not yours—may engage in risky behavior is not helpful. This attitude can actually put your daughter in jeopardy.

There are many ways you can mitigate these challenges. Young women who have support to resist conforming to rigid sex roles have opportunities to develop persistence and a variety of skills and become self-confident and resilient. You can strengthen your daughter's confidence by encouraging her to know and practice her core values and to be true to herself.

When you do too much for your daughter, you give her the message that you don't believe she can do things or make decisions on her own. Giving her the message that you believe she is developing the skills she needs to make the best choices for herself is an important part of letting go. Recognize your daughter's strengths, and help her to acknowledge them. You can help her work toward crafting a life where she relies on her strengths and addresses her weaknesses. Girls have to know how to set goals for themselves, develop healthy relationships, handle internal emotions, and not depend primarily on outside evaluations.

Some girls cope well with stress; others do not. Substance abuse, reckless and violent behavior, and suicide are some examples of destructive coping mechanisms. One of your objectives should be to provide your daughter with positive ways of coping, which may include physical exercise, writing in journals, talking to friends and family members, or reducing the number of activities in which she is involved. Practicing these positive coping techniques will serve your daughter well for the rest of her life. By building competent spheres based on core values (consisting of the family values that she has internalized and accepted as her own), your daughter will be able to create a strong sense of self, one that will allow her to meet the challenges of the teenage years.

OBSTACLES AND BARRIERS TO ACHIEVEMENT AND SELF-ESTEEM

It may be helpful for you to identify successful and unsuccessful resolutions to challenges in your daughter's life. Concrete examples may be instructive in guiding your daughter to overcome future obstacles. You can use these examples to demonstrate to your daughter what has worked or not worked for her in the past.

Identify a challenge and briefly describe the resolution that may have affected your daughter's self-esteem and/or ability to achieve:

Elementary School
Challenge:

Resolution: What happened? Was it a satisfactory resolution or not?

Middle School
Challenge:

Resolution: What happened? Was it a satisfactory resolution or not?

High School
Challenge:

Resolution: What happened? Was it a satisfactory resolution or not?

Focus on Adolescent Girls of Color

"My parents once said that there is nothing so gratifying as breaking a stereotype, and I have come to believe that this is true. I never really realized how many people that I have changed in my life. I have changed teachers who dared to assume that I would never excel in their classes because of the color of my skin. I have changed the minds of adults who thought that I would be rude and brash just because I am black.... I truly believe that all of the hatred in this world stems from fear of what we do not know. I think we all need to gain the courage to overcome our fears. Only then can we actually know, appreciate, and love our fellow man, regardless of external appearance."

—NNEKA NNOAKE UFERE, 14, Iris Jacob's
My Sisters' Voices: Teenage Girls of Color Speak Out

Our discussions with girls of color and their families demonstrate that there is not one girl culture, but several, frequently with different struggles, different perceptions of school, and different views about standards of beauty, peer pressure, and family. Teenage girls agree, however, they are forced to grow up too fast as they face an environment filled with drugs and alcohol, the pressure to "fit in" and to have sex, sexual harassment, impossible standards of beauty, and, as one 15-year-old said, "little time to be kids." In addition to their similar perceptions, Dr. Harriette Pipes McAdoo of Howard University is quoted in Barbara Warren-Sams's 2001 article, "Mentors Confirm and Enhance Girls' Lives," as saying that young women of color share certain experiences, including the following:

* Seeing the world differently from white girls, regardless of their social class
* Experiencing devaluation of their talents because they are from groups that have been traditionally less appreciated by mainstream society
* Feeling peer pressure to reject success when measured by white standards
* Having extended relationships with family and friends that involve a larger network of caring adults and increased responsibilities for younger children

According to the 2000 U.S. Census Bureau, "Current Population Survey," girls of color account for more than a third of teenage girls. African-Americans, Latinas, Asian-Americans, and Native American girls grow up in cultures based in part on an expectation of a lifelong attachment to family and community. European-American girls grow up in a culture that values family but places great emphasis on independence and autonomy. Many girls of color have greater responsibility within their homes, including the care of younger siblings. School is considered to be only one part of their education: "Indeed, formal education is often perceived as secondary to a humanistic education that centers on loyalty, respect, and integrity," says Julia Potter in her article "Building Bridges Between Cultures." These differences in expectations filter mainstream culture through a different lens.

Identity: Self-Image, Ethnicity, and Gender

Girls of color develop their identity within the context of their racial or ethnic group. Seventeen-year-old Alicia, a Latina, said, "I feel even stronger when I achieve something because of my identity. It gives me strength when someone tells me I can't do something. I try to prove I can." Many girls of color experience rejection because of race, ethnicity, and culture or a combination of gender and these other factors. This experience of double discrimination can be destructive to both the individual and the group.

Girls of color learn at an early age about the impact of stereotyping. It is confusing for them to try to establish an identity from what they read in the mass media and see in the movies and on television. Seventeen-year-old Akeisha observed, "What we see on television and in magazines is totally different from what we see at home and with our families. It's very hard to break away from the clutches of what society decides is acceptable. But, as an African-American, I have no choice but to turn away from outside sources that tell me who I am supposed to be." As a result, some girls of color develop an oppositional identity in response to a culture that doesn't include their unique American experience.

Culturally dissonant pressures, expectations, and conflicts among home, community, school, and mainstream culture may promote mis-

"Deborah Roberts, ABC News Correspondent, shares, 'Uppermost in my mind with my daughter is making sure she's equipped with confidence. She's already noticing the difference in her skin and the other girls' lighter skin. I want her to feel wonderful about who she is, and I want my son to appreciate his sister and all women in all shades.'"

—ALLISON SAMUELS, "Time to Tell It Like It Is"

informed, unhealthy, and unfair choices for adolescents from diverse ethnic and cultural backgrounds. For example, from childhood, Latinas are taught to be obedient, respectful, industrious, virtuous, and religious. They are expected to integrate these values and adhere to them throughout their lifetime. During adolescence, the daughter in a Latino family is frequently protected and sheltered. Because of the importance of maintaining traditional cultural values, Latinas may experience contradictory messages from their families about achieving success in the mainstream culture.

Unlike many European-American families, most Latino families allow for different social privileges based on gender as sons and daughters grow older. One mother explained, "I work a 40-hour week, as does my husband. In our family I'm expected to get dinner on the table and take care of the kids more than my Anglo friends. Sometimes I wonder how my daughter will respond to the message that she should be an equal in her future family, yet that's not what she sees in our house."

Asian-American girls are expected to be respectful, be high achievers, and have strong family bonds throughout their life. Frequently, middle-class African-American girls who have the skills to adjust to mainstream culture feel pressure to adapt to that culture and devalue their own culture in the process. These types of cultural values and sex role socializations affect girls' interpretations of both in-school and out-of-school experiences.

Mixed Signals

The media and mainstream culture play a central role in adolescent development and can shape a girl's sense of herself. One mother said, "I'm worried because so many teenage girls define themselves by the music and what they see on the videos. I'm young enough to remember that parents never appreciate their children's music, but I can't get past the 'bitches,' 'hos,' and misogyny. They see what's 'in' and what's popular and just adopt street life and the hip-hop culture lifestyle and apply it to their own lives."

Vanessa, mother of 18-year-old Sukari, also expressed concern about the number of hours of rap videos and music her daughter watches and listens to. Vanessa said, "I don't like the way rap talks about women. Men hold all the power, and women don't. The violence and disrespect get to me. I know why she likes it, but the message is all wrong." Media have a tremendous impact on the formation of beliefs and attitudes. It's important for you to know what your daughter is watching because, according to Susan Buttross of the American Academy of Pediatrics, in "Study Finds Link Between Rap Videos and Violence," "We know that with any type of repeated media exposure, a desensitization may occur that makes these behaviors seem [almost] normal."

The television family hour, the 8:00 to 9:00 hour, is the "whitest time" of television. Therefore, it's not surprising that girls of color hunger for images that look like them. These children feel ambushed by the images they see on television. African-American girls, for the most part, seem to be able to resist the negativity and hold onto their self-esteem, even though they are bombarded with stereotypical imagery. The credit goes to their parents and other adult role models who continually affirm who they are. One mother said, "I tell my daughter, 'I like your assertiveness. You are beautiful. I love you.' My husband would ask our daughter, 'Who are you?' and she would respond, 'I'm the most beautiful, most brilliant girl in the world.'" These kinds of messages go a long way in building resilient and competent young women.

Too often we try to hold everybody to one standard for what is beautiful. When we do that we deny ourselves the opportunity to appreciate the beauty to be found in the majority of the world's population. In spite of these messages, the good news is that universally, girls of color are more satisfied with their bodies and shapes than are white girls. Girls of color, says Paula Span in her article "It's a Girl's World," "are no less concerned about their appearances, but their standards of beauty are more flexible and go beyond the physical to include a personal sense of style, self-confidence, and attitude."

Many of the girls we spoke with felt good about themselves, in spite of experiencing rejection in their lives as a result of race, ethnicity, and/or gender. When asked about how they feel about themselves, they responded, "I'm proud of who I am"; "I'm strong"; and "I can do anything." Many African-American families are more worried about boys and men of color. The girls talked about "women overpowering the men." The men "are being dissed." They know that women of color are victimized by race and gender bias, but they are particularly concerned about what is happening to their male counterparts. Young men of color appear to have greater difficulty maintaining a positive self-image.

Girls of color benefit from cultures that allow for variation in body type, but, at the same time, they still suffer from the monolithic white standards of beauty perpetuated in the media and advertisements. We are all victims of the manipulation of popular culture. For example, *Essence*, a magazine that caters to middle-class African-American women, regularly runs stories on body size, anxiety, and eating disorders, a fact that suggests that conventional white standards become more relevant among women of color as affluence increases.

African-American girls learn that a woman with fairly light skin and long hair has the "power to make others see her as popular and attractive." One woman remembered, in high school, some of the darker-skinned students even taunted her: "You think you bad 'cuz you got some hair?" Many of the African-American girls we spoke with discussed the prejudice they feel because of being darker skinned: "You kinda cute for a dark-skinned girl."

Obesity is a major problem among all races and ethnicities. Black girls are twice as likely as white girls to be overweight based on the white body image standard of model thin. As one mother said, "Obesity is killing our daughters softly." According to Jodi Lipson, at the Sister-to-Sister summit facilitated by the American Association of University Women, teenage girls had the following reactions to the "idealized," white standard of beauty:

"There's this girl in that Calvin Klein commercial—she's so skinny! It's nice to see healthy girls. She looks deadly anorexic, bulimic. She looks like she has a terminal illness. That's the representation they want us to achieve. It makes me furious. They expect us to look like that. She looks scary; she looks like a skeleton. It makes me pissed. They can't find someone healthy? I'm supposed to look like that? Can she run? Can she jump?"

"Do you see yourself in magazines? No. They're all so thin. It just hurts your feelings. I try to be thin but I can't. I can just be the way I am."

Another young African-American woman described dealing with her "robust posterior," "in an age in which everything is shrinking—government, computers, distances between peoples"—calling it "butt reckoning."

Catching the Right Educational Train

Girls and women of color continue to experience bias in educational settings. Female African-American and Latina students reported to us that they must cope with innuendo and body language that suggest they don't measure up. One mother described how the combination of race and gender discrimination affects both her daughter's classroom instruction and the academic and career counseling her daughter receives. She reported, "I personally know of African-American mothers who had to make visits to school to change their daughters' schedules from those proposed by the counselors to ones that included required college prep courses. The counselors justified their course selection for these girls based on their presumption that girls of color would find the courses too difficult. These girls went on to succeed in their [advanced placement] classes. My own daughter was guided away from advanced science and math courses until she insisted that she take these courses to prepare for engineering school." In addition to looking out for inappropriate course selections by the schools, parents of children of color must be vigilant to make sure their daughters do not self-select less challenging courses because they have internalized external sources of discouragement.

Researchers hypothesize that negative stereotypes may lead to heightened self-consciousness at the very same time that adolescents develop abstract reasoning and an understanding of the world around them. Teenage cognitive development makes their awareness of unfair treatment unavoidable. Adolescents are developing a new understanding of their own capacity to make decisions and choices, and they are beginning to focus on identity development. Unfortunately, as students of color become more aware of racism, they may identify school as a hostile environment.

Adolescent girls from diverse ethnic and cultural groups are often forced to choose between their racial/ethnic and cultural group identity and attainment of traditional "success," as defined by academic achievement and peer group membership. African-American children may come to believe that to preserve and promote the value of their own identity, they must reject academic achievement. This is the direct result of inadequate exposure to positive role models and to the rich history of African-American intellectualism as well as these children being tracked disproportionately into lower-level academic programs. Participating in high-level courses may mean leaving friends behind.

Lola, age 18, reported, "I was hurrying to class one day when I was stopped in the hall by a group of my friends. One girl said to me, 'Who do you think you are? A black girl trying to be white. Do you think you are better than us? School won't get you anywhere. Girl, you're racing to class like some white chick. Wouldn't you rather be with us?'"

A parent told of her familiarity with this same conflict when she talked with us about the experience of Latinas. Maria, the mother of 17-year-old Delores, told us, "A Spanish kid is not expected to do well. I'm constantly telling her to do her best. If she doesn't do her best, it's not good enough. My daughter fights with us about homework. She wants to hang out with her friends. It's a constant struggle to support both her academic achievement and her comfort with her group of friends, especially her Latino friends." As long as success is defined by school and peer groups as "white," achievement will continue to be a source of conflict for girls of color. Educators contribute to this conflict when they have lower expectations for girls of color and steer them into easier classes. Parents can mitigate these challenges by having high expectations for their daughters and supporting their achievement in school.

The experience of girls of color in addressing racism is different during their school years. For example, according to the American Association of University Women, in *Gender Gaps: Where Schools Still Fail Our Children*, African-American girls enter school assertive, confident, and outgoing; they grow more passive and quiet through the school years. Because of this progressive silencing, some African-American girls feel compelled to adopt "attitude" to develop an identity and obtain respect in school.

One African-American girl described her reasons for adopting this "attitude." Florence said, "It lets people know that I'm serious, that I'm not playing, and it's a good way, you know, for people to listen, to know that I'm trying to get a point across." This choice of voice may strike some of us as a negative response to tough issues, but many African-American girls feel it is necessary to encourage people to acknowledge and listen to them.

Rita, an 11th grader in a public school, "is acknowledged to be a brilliant student, but all her teachers and many of her peers worry about her because she presents a 'polyrhymic, nonsymmetrical, non-linear' persona. She is bold and sassy, creative, complex, and indeflatable. She frequently challenges the values and rules of the school with conviction. . . ." In the article "Those Loud Black Girls," Signithia Fordham goes on to say that Rita is able to function in both the academic world and her culture of origin. Her articulate arguments feel like badgering to some of her teachers, because she says and does everything with "attitude." Rita doesn't follow rules, but because she gets her work done, she gets rewarded. She refuses to be deferential, even when the school system demands it. Adolescent girls, especially girls of color from low-income families, realize that unless they speak up, they will be offered little from a society that frequently discounts them.

When they enter high school, all students must cope with a dramatic increase in the size of their school, the structure of academic schedules, and the complexity of school environments. Faced with new academic demands, fewer supports, negative messages from school, few academic role models, and the uncertain payoff of school, some students turn away from academics. Once again, we do not know why others persevere. Some hypothesize that the primary encouraging factors are parental expectations and involvement.

Research indicates that during their school years, African-American girls frequently are steered toward an acceptable black female social role. Because black girls are looked on by teachers as mature, self-reliant, and helpful, they are often expected to serve as a "social integrator," bringing children from all different backgrounds together. On the other hand, because of cultural bias regarding their academic abilities, African-American girls are denied the proper attention and recognition necessary to encourage their intellectual achievement. For example, their comments in class discussions may be ignored, and they may not receive the help they need in academics. This duality encourages the development of social skills at the expense of academic skills.

As a result of racial and cultural bias and peer group influence, African-American girls may lack academic self-confidence, have lower opinions of their teachers and schoolwork than girls of any other group, and gradually become angry with and alienated from the academic system. Black girls attempt to initiate interaction more than all children, regardless of race; however, teachers resist these efforts disproportionately, and young black women receive little reinforcement for their performance.

The cultural expectations of Latina and Asian girls include feminine characteristics that produce behavior acceptable within the school culture. For example, Latinas are expected to demonstrate "demure behavior and deference to authority, . . ." observes Lisa Dietrich in *Chicana Adolescents*. Unfortunately, while Latina behavior is appropriate for school, the educational system's expectations for their academic achievement is so low that many of them feel discouraged from even trying to perform. Among all racial and cultural groups, Latinas have the highest dropout rates. A total of 23.5 percent of Latinas, 11.1 percent of African-American girls, and 6.9 percent of white girls dropped out of high school in 2001. Pregnancy and/or parenting are the leading reasons girls give for dropping out of school. Specific factors seem to influence more female dropouts than male, including having a large number of siblings, their mother's educational level, low academic achievement, and low self-esteem, according to *Dropout Rates in the United States* from the U.S. Department of Education.

Other factors that contribute to Latina underachievement include their responsibilities for taking care of younger family members and conflicting cultural expectations for female social roles. Latinas are caught in a vicious cycle: what is expected from them culturally may conflict with their academic achievement. The lack of teacher intervention contributes to their alienation from school. Latinas' alienation, in turn, discourages teachers from intervening on their behalf. Many of the Latinas with whom we spoke find little to identify with in the school community. They lack the role models and access to multicultural curriculum that might engage their interest.

The conflict between traditional cultural roots and success as a student also affects Asian-American girls, but in a different way. Asian-American cultural expectations of behavior for girls conform to those expected at school. As a result, Asian students are expected to be "model students." In fact, they often exceed the achievement of white students. As a result, other students of color sometimes harass them because they are perceived as trying to be "white." However, not all Asian students do well in school. Those in need may receive little help in overcoming their academic difficulties because they tend to be quiet and compliant and are presumed to be doing well. Asian girls also must wrestle with cultural conflicts between home and school life.

Julia, 17 years old, reported, "I feel I have a split life; school encourages opinions and open-mindedness, and at home I am discouraged from expressing opinions that differ from [those of] my parents. My brother can be more opinionated. I have to just go along. At school, I'm expected to speak out; yet, at home I'm taught that speaking out is disrespectful. It's a good thing I do well on exams and papers, because I'm not comfortable to express my own views."

The pressure to be perfect is also a factor that many Asian girls agree is extremely stressful. Connie, mother of 16-year-old Minh, reported, "My daughter is constantly under pressure to perform well in all of her subjects. She does do well in math and science, but [she] is not the best writer. When she speaks up in class to get help, the teacher assumes she is just trying to get attention, and so do the kids. I want her to do well in school, but I also want her to be comfortable. She doesn't have to be the best at everything."

Asian-American girls are beginning to articulate their concerns and to explore their options. They want to be good students, but as one Asian-American girl put it, "We want to have an 'edge,' just like any other teen. We want to have the freedom to make mistakes and act out." Asian-American girls are developing their own voices as they work at becoming more comfortable in both cultures. Their emerging voices represent an integration of cultures. We hope this integration will have an overall positive effect, because it will increase communication between parents and children, in school, and among peers.

The Path to Success: The Role of Parents

The achievement of students of color is influenced by a complex combination of institutional, class, gender, and identity issues. Success in school begins at home. Parents with whom we spoke agreed that keeping girls on track requires parental vigilance, high academic expectations, encouragement to participate in sports and church activities, availability of after-school programs, and a disciplined social life. These parents do not hesitate to tell their daughters about the value of education, the importance of financial independence, and the risks of the street. These parents also understand institutional racism and the enormous social pressure on their daughters to *not* succeed.

Carolyn, mother of 16-year-old Sharonda, told us, "I keep telling my daughter that if she graduates and goes to college it would pay off. I don't have a college degree, and I know it's a must for her. There are so many ways she can get into trouble in my neighborhood. People are hanging out at all hours, and young people are up to no good, drinking and smoking weed. Sharonda is always asking me why she can't do things like her other friends. I keep going back to education. I know it's even harder for all the single mothers who are trying to keep their daughters focused. I say keep them busy with church and sports. Keep them too busy to get into trouble. But they still get into trouble, even with support from parents. It's just hard."

The girls we spoke with echoed these sentiments. Thirteen-year-old Brenda reported, "I try to remember what my mother says, 'listen to what I say, not what everybody else says, 'cause it's their opinion.'" The girls know they can't do it alone, and they rely on their families and each other to counteract the negative influences many of their peers can't resist. These girls also have the added pressure of society telling them they are being successful at the expense of boys of color. As Ellis Cose said in a recent *Newsweek* article, "The Black Gender Gap," "When talk turns to Black women's triumphs, it generally segues

"In times of rapid cultural change . . . strong ties with family elders sustain access to wisdom and cultural traditions."
—CATHERINE COOPER, JILL DENNER, and EDWARD LOPEZ,
"Cultural Brokers: Helping Latino Children on Toward Success"

to the failure of Black men to keep up." This reality offers girls another burden to carry.

Resistance and Resiliency

Family, family, family is what strengthens girls and enables them to combat the racism they inevitably face in society. Parents and other family members who provide suggestions for dealing with bias and emphasize individual achievement and self-efficacy raise daughters who can distinguish between roles that are imposed by society and their own self-definition. They raise daughters who, as author bell hooks writes in *Black Looks: Race and Representation*, can succeed in a society where prejudice is still prevalent. Therefore, "when messages of white society say 'you can't,' the well-functioning Black family and community stand ready to counter such messages with those that say, 'You can, we have, we will.'" Erika, 16 years old, said, "Whenever I would tell my parents how funny I felt being one of the few of my friends to constantly raise my hand in class to contribute, my dad would say, 'Erika, you just keep shooting that hand up. Participating won't hurt you. You'll be seen and you won't be forgotten. Keep your hand up and your head high.'"

The identification girls of color share with their families and ethnic/racial groups provides strength and resources in a society that continues to marginalize them. Sharing common values, language, and history serves to vaccinate girls against the destruction of racial and gender discrimination. In fact, the degree to which girls of color incorporate positive messages about their culture and history helps to influence their healthy development. A divided identity works against girls creating self-confidence and self-efficacy. When girls integrate positive messages about their culture, they build resiliency and the strength to have faith in themselves, even, and most especially, when others don't believe in them.

LOOKING BACK

Use a blank piece of paper or a journal and the following statements to help you remember what your teenage years were like. This exercise can help provide you with insight and build empathy for your daughter. Remembering the past helps you to better understand what it's like being in a teenager's shoes.

* Describe an event or circumstance that left a deep impression on you.
* Consider the role your race/ethnicity, culture, social class, and gender played in this event.
* Think about how the event might have been altered if you were of a different race/ethnicity, culture, social class, or gender than you are.

5

Making the Transition

The Experiences of Everyday School Life

"For school we got an open mind, good grades, participation, we've got the attitude, a certain perspective. You have to suck up sometimes, you have to be quiet, you have to know certain people, you have to try to be yourself, you have to be attentive, on task, you have to study a lot. And for the crowd you have to wear the right clothes, you have to have the attitude, you have to be willing to bully people, you also have to suck up to like your friends or whatever, you have to be outgoing, daring, you have to know certain people, and sometimes you have to be mean."

—Written by an adolescent girl and quoted in
Research for Action, Inc.'s *Girls in the Middle:
Working to Succeed in School*

Parents often have difficulty deciphering the secret lives of their teenage daughters. Knowing when to step in and when to allow children to be more independent is a difficult call. However, your attitude toward education and involvement in the school life of your daughter is extremely critical to her academic achievement. It's important that you're aware of what you can and should expect from the schools your daughter attends. These expectations certainly include providing your daughter with a safe learning environment—emotionally and intellectually. Your actions and involvement play a central role in your daughter's sex-role socialization and educational experience, and your choices and attitudes about activities, friendships, and academic achievement can shape (or skew) her sense of self.

In this chapter, we explore the dynamics of school life and how they affect girls. The most salient issues include the pursuit of academic achievement, the influence of peer groups and sports, the impact of sexual harassment and bullying, and the challenges of being a nontraditional girl. Creating safe and equitable schools depends greatly on adults effectively transmitting and modeling the emotional support, caring, and consistent expectations so critical to girls' development. In addition, girls themselves must have the opportunity to develop positive self-esteem, learn about and be respectful toward others, and be held accountable for their behavior.

Great Expectations: Girls' Academic Achievement

Barbara, the mother of four teenage daughters, remembered her experience in school: "My parents insisted that I attend college. 'After all,' they repeated, 'no college-educated man will want to marry you if you don't have a diploma.' I enrolled at San Francisco State University, where I became interested in psychology. Like so many women of my generation, I was given a choice between teaching and nursing. I chose teaching, with the hope that, maybe someday, I could become a guidance counselor. My parents told me that was a good choice because, 'You can always earn a little extra money substitute teaching' or 'Teaching was a job that I could always fall back on!'

"My education was never meant to support a lifelong career, but rather it was geared toward a temporary job that I held long enough to put my husband through medical school. Despite my academic achievements, my role was to live vicariously through the accomplishments of my husband and children. Thank goodness the times have changed for my daughters."

Thirty-plus years after the passage of Title IX, the federal law that prohibits gender discrimination in education, many researchers have reflected on both the legislative progress and continued barriers. Richard W. Riley, former U.S. Secretary of Education, quoted in the U.S. Department of Education's *Title IX: 25 Years of Progress*, noted, "What strikes me the most about the progress that has been achieved since Title IX was passed in 1972 is that there has been a sea change in our expectations of what women [and girls] can achieve."

Girls have increased the kinds and numbers of courses they take in high school, and they are scoring higher on standardized tests. The Women's Educational Equity Act Resource Center reported in 2000 that girls are choosing more classes based on their interests and skills rather than on traditionally presumed or identified gender roles. Girls are more likely to enroll in college immediately following high school, and by 2007, universities are projected to enroll 9.2 million women and 6.9 million men, says Anna Mulrine in a 2001 *U.S. News and World Report* article. There is no question that Title IX has opened wide some doors previously closed to women and girls. However, barriers still exist and must be addressed in collaboration between parents and school staff.

Classroom Climate

In the classroom, instances of gender bias and discrimination are manifested in three ways and often go unrecognized. First, girls are simply left out. For example, teachers call on boys more often than they do on girls, and girls are often rewarded for being compliant and quiet. In *Title IX at 30*, the National Coalition for Women and Girls in Education states that boys demand and receive more attention from teachers and counselors for their positive and negative behaviors. A teacher reports: "Part of my tendency to respond to the boys first was a behavior management concern. While the girls were sitting respect-fully raising their hands, the boys were having difficulty controlling their behavior; they were wildly raising their hands, spilling their solutions and knocking over their test tubes. So calling on them first helped them to stay focused and keep their experiment intact." By giving these boys more attention, the teacher sent an unintended message to the girls—their classroom contributions are less important.

Many girls covet more academic interaction and "real-life" discussions with their teachers. This appeal runs counter to the stereotypical notion that teenagers want to be left alone and don't want adults involved in their lives. Classroom interaction builds girls' cognitive competence, and it's a teacher's responsibility to keep girls involved.

Second, informal surveys of teachers and counselors found that they view girls who question, challenge, and actively interact with teachers and other students as aggressive, power-hungry, and emotional (now sometimes referred to as "alpha girls," says Rosalind Wiseman in *Queen Bees and Wannabes*), while the same behavior demonstrated by boys is cast in a positive light. One 17-year-old girl told us how her teacher makes girls feel uncomfortable about being "too outspoken." This teacher, who also coaches the baseball team, jokes around with the guys for half the class period but becomes antagonistic or sarcastic whenever one of the girls asks a question or raises a concern.

The third instance of gender bias can be found in the standard curriculum. The problem is not a lack of information about the contributions of women and people of color, it's that the information isn't included or accessed. In one example of 1,000 pages of a U.S. history text, less than 3 percent of the history was about women. The result?

"When asked, most students cannot name twenty famous women from American history. Typically, they list fewer than five," reports the National Coalition for Women and Girls in Education in 2002.

People of color and women are often relegated to sidebars, bibliographies, addenda, and appendixes. In history, mathematics, literature, and the sciences, the influence of women is rarely evident (or examined). Leslie, a 17-year-old high school student, noted, "I've been in honors classes throughout my high school career and have had almost no knowledge of what women contributed to these disciplines." Contemporary curricula continue to hide facts that could benefit the self-esteem of girls and help to eliminate sexist attitudes and behaviors of males toward females.

Boys and girls are bombarded with overt and covert messages about what they can be and do based on their gender. Although there have been many changes in the past three decades, there is still work to be done. Because the messages concerning appropriate roles for females and males have become more subtle (the hidden curriculum), many teachers and students have more difficulty recognizing gender bias in the classroom. The first step toward changing inequities in school is raising awareness. Parents must be aware of sexism to counter pervasive gender stereotypes that affect their daughters' success. Teachers need to make a conscious effort to provide girls and boys with an equitable learning environment so that all students can achieve to the best of their abilities.

Self-Esteem and Academic Achievement

Something actually happens to many girls when they enter middle school that affects their academic achievement. Research for Action, Inc., in *Girls in the Middle*, reports that girls who were once outspoken, willing to take risks, and self-confident experience a general decline in school performance. For example, according to the National Center for Education Statistics' 2000 and 2002 editions of *National Assessment of Educational Progress*, girls exhibit a general decline in science achievement beginning in middle school. As reported in *Title IX at 30*, this gap increases in high school, and women continue to be underrepresented in science and math in higher education.

These middle school years are the times when being popular and fitting in too frequently take precedence over being assertive and competent and taking academic risks. Risking failure or standing out too much increases girls' psychological barriers to achievement. Karen, a senior in high school, remembered: "Saying what I really thought got me into trouble with teachers and with my friends. I was always on the verge of some disaster. I was a bitch if I spoke out, especially if I was willing to argue with boys, and my teachers always presented me as 'challenging' to my parents at back-to-school nights."

As girls move into high school, some of these conflicts are masked because girls continue to get better grades than boys and are the subject of fewer disciplinary actions. This may be one of the few rewards female students receive for their compliant classroom behavior; however, their conformity comes at the cost of self-esteem and achievement as measured by standardized tests (such as the SAT), independence, and self-reliance. The following story illustrates two parents' determination to help their daughter resist outdated stereotyped expectations. Jo told us:

> When our daughter, Lara, was in high school, she was extremely reluctant to speak out in class. In fact, she refused to wear red (a color that accentuates her dark hair and coloring) to school because it made her more noticeable. . . . One history teacher notified the students that they couldn't receive a grade of A if they didn't participate in class. This teacher was notorious for "pushing" students

when they gave an answer. Many students were not used to this type of give-and-take and wouldn't answer in class.

Our daughter, with her reticent nature, would have been quite content to sit back and listen. . . . She was in tears at home. She'd say, "I can't talk in there. All those debaters know everything. All those debaters are boys. I'll feel like an idiot if I'm wrong." We asked her if she would rather get a B even though she knew the material perfectly. She decided she wanted to try to participate. We helped her set goals. At first she had to volunteer a certain number of times per week. Then it was a set number of times per day. We told her we didn't care if she got the answers wrong, all she had to do was talk, and we would pay her the magnificent sum of one dollar for each interaction. She laughed at our cheap reward, but she was sufficiently motivated to try the scheme.

There were many days when she came home in tears because she just couldn't make herself raise her hand. Finally, she forced herself to take the plunge on a regular basis, and by the end of the semester she was participating freely and even received a comment on her report card that she "participates well in class"; this was next to her grade—an A. Lara's academic career was one of extraordinary accomplishment. After graduating at the top of her high school class, she attended Princeton, graduated magna cum laude as a physics major, and went on to do graduate work in biophysics.

But without their parental vigilance and willingness to intervene, Lara's mother suspects that her daughter's story might not have had such a positive ending.

Parents have to work with schools to examine the messages that lead girls to believe that fitting in, looks, and popularity, rather than intelligence and accomplishment, will enable them to succeed. We also need to look beyond whether boys and girls are allowed the same quality and variety of learning opportunities.

HOW DOES YOUR DAUGHTER LEARN BEST?

We can best help our daughters in school by knowing how they learn "best." Ask your daughter questions such as, "Do you like working independently and thinking for yourself?" or "Do you like to work with a friend or friends as part of a team?" "Do you learn best by creating something?" or "Do you learn best by listening?" "Do you learn best by looking at a map?" or "Do you learn best when someone writes out directions?"

LEARNING STRENGTHS

* If she learns best when she listens, she may be an auditory learner.
* If she learns best when she looks at something, she may be a visual learner.
* If she learns best by doing things, she may be a kinesthetic learner.

In addition to learning strengths, your daughter may prefer one type of learning over another. Review the following categories to further understand her learning preferences.

LEARNING TYPES

Field Independent
* Learning is abstract and analytical.
* Learning is not necessarily related to environment, experience, and personality.
* Learning is individual- and teacher-centered.

Field Sensitive
* Learning is related to environment, experience, and personality.
* Personal and social impact is important, as are practical values.
* Attention needs to be paid to contextual field.

continued

continued ▮

* One is sensitive to personal dynamics and criticism.
* Learning is cooperative and group- or peer-centered.

Compare what your daughter told you about her learning preferences and how she works best with your own observations. Using this information only as a guide, try to encourage your daughter to lead with her strengths while also trying to improve in areas that she finds more challenging. You may want to share this information with your daughter's teachers.

Flirting with Danger: Sexual Harassment at School

Sexual harassment is a problem that affects both genders. It often starts in elementary school with teasing or other inappropriate remarks regarding another's body as well as bullying and playground rough-housing. Although the impact of sexual harassment is greater on girls, boys also experience harassment. Same-sex harassment, especially with taunts related to homosexuality, is common.

Eighty percent of students say they have encountered some form of sexual harassment. A sexual harassment experience seems to have an effect on students' educational, emotional, and physical development, with girls reporting more problems than boys.

Though schools have policies against it, sexual harassment remains an all-too-common problem. About 70 percent of students say their schools have rules related to harassment, compared with 26 percent in 1993, according to a survey given initially by the American Association of University Women in 1998 and again in 2001. While students say they are aware of school policies dealing with sexual harassment, increased awareness has not always translated into school life. Kara, a middle school girl, said, "Policies just don't stick." Parents and educators need to do a better job of educating students about what is and isn't appropriate school behavior.

In simplest terms, sexual harassment is deliberate and/or repeated sexual or sex-based behavior that is not welcome and is not asked for. It may be any of the following:

* Physical, such as unwelcome touching or interference with movement
* Verbal, such as epithets, derogatory comments or slurs, the spread of sexual gossip, or pressure for dates and/or sexual activity
* Visual, such as displaying derogatory cartoons, drawings, posters, or messages

A hostile situation usually involves a series of incidents that poison the environment by creating an offensive, intimidating climate that interferes with work performance and academic achievement. Consider the following examples:

Denise, a seventh grader, goes to the counselor's office in tears. It seems that Max, an eighth grader, waits for her in the cafeteria each day. He persists in standing behind her, patting her backside, and asking her personal questions. Max asks, "Are you still a virgin?" "How would you like to do it with me for your first time?" Some of Denise's friends think she should be flattered by the attention. After all, Max is very good looking, bright, and popular. In spite of what her friends say, Denise is intimidated by his attention.

In a suburban middle school during the time when students are moving from one class to another, several male students seem to make a point of brushing up against female students and making physical contact. Occasionally, an angry female student will report the incident. When this happens, male students accuse her of being a poor sport or say she's making a big deal out of it.

During lunch, female students walk down the hallway to their lockers. Male students frequently congregate along the hallway and make comments about the girls' appearance as they pass. They rate the girls on a scale of 1 to 10.

A teacher shared the following story that took place in her high school U.S. history class: "I called on one of the female students to answer a question. Just as she began to speak, she slammed her hand down on her desk, turned around to face the male student sitting behind her, and shouted, 'Stop that! Don't say things right behind my head so I can't think and can't answer the question!' He said, 'I didn't say anything.' She answered, 'You always say terrible things just behind my head so the teacher can't tell that you're doing it.' I moved the male student to the one vacant seat in the front of the room for the rest of the period and talked with him after class. Until the one brave female student made me aware of this type of harassment, I had not been aware that it was taking place!"

Girls can also be harassers. One parent shared the following incident involving her son: "Rob recently transferred to a new high school. He passed through the art corridor, a favorite hangout of the older girls. Lydia and her friends, Leticia and Mary, ranked Rob as he passed by. Rob overheard Lydia say, 'Can't wait to undress you,' while Leticia patted Rob's butt and commented, 'Nice butt. Can I photograph you for my project?' Mary laughed the whole time, and other students who were nearby, both male and female, started coming closer to see and hear what was going on. Rob mumbled something under his breath and quickly continued down the hall. He was mortified and avoided that area whenever possible.

"At first, I told Rob that this was just part of high school life and not to take it personally. But after repeated incidents, I went to the counselor. Rob didn't want to get the kids in trouble. As a new kid in school, he knew that would be the end of him. The counselor helped Rob practice various responses to the harassment. After a while, it worked, but I'm sure the girls went on to torment other victims."

If your teens are courageous enough to tell you about incidents that cause them intense pain or embarrassment, you need to be careful not to dismiss the behavior as "boys will be boys" and "girls will be girls." If you trivialize such incidents—if not actually condone them—girls and boys learn to mistrust adults and environments that should protect them.

Often perceived as "normal" adolescent behavior, sexual harassment persists as a social problem. Such behaviors may set the stage for date or acquaintance rape. Parents and school officials cannot afford to ignore signals of distress or deny the issues altogether, and complaints must be pursued with vigilance.

Although we have come to associate acquaintance or date rape with college campuses, it happens to high school girls as well. Estimates of violence among high school students range from 10 percent to 25 percent. If one includes verbal threats and emotional abuse, the estimates are even higher, according to the 2003 article, "Dating Violence." Acquaintance rape is sometimes difficult to define and may be confused with "normal" male behavior. If date rape is difficult for adults to define, then it is even harder for young people, who are just beginning to understand the complexities of sexual relationships.

Although schools cannot control what happens to students outside of school, schools and the courts are grappling with the responsibility of schools for off-campus but school-related activities. Parents and educators can help boys and girls to understand that acquaintance rape is a form of violence against women and girls, rather than minimizing the violence or making excuses for the perpetrator. Educators should promote a school climate based on respect and dignity, and parents must model that behavior for their children and expect them to behave accordingly.

At a minimum, schools must inform parents and students about the school district's sexual harassment policies and codes for student conduct. They should also indicate the proper person(s) in the school with whom to talk if parents suspect their child is being harassed. It is important to acknowledge that, in many cases, harassers engage in behaviors that they never learned were inappropriate. Stereotypical images of men and women perpetuate interactions that stress conflict with the other sex as well as within the same sex, particularly if the boy or girl "doesn't fit in," or doesn't meet traditional stereotypes.

This socialization process begins early in life. By the time a child has reached the teen years, sexist attitudes are well embedded. Societal myths tell teenage boys what is expected of them—to be macho, in control, dominant, and aggressive. Males think females want constant sexual attention, and conquering a female is necessary to build the male ego. Females are considered to be sex objects (check out the teenage pornographic websites that creep into your computers if you have any doubts about that) and are encouraged to believe that males can't help themselves and that their libidos are out of control. Or girls don't feel good about themselves if boys do not want them (romantically or sexually). These sexist attitudes encourage incidents of sexual harassment.

It is in everyone's best interests to help our children develop healthy sexuality at an early age and to intervene when we see inappropriate behavior at home and at school. By intervening, we can support both the perpetrator(s) and the victim(s) to get appropriate help. The harm caused by sexual harassment and abuse doesn't end with high school graduation. Young women and men take their experiences to college campuses and the workplace, where the detrimental effects of sexual harassment continue to take a toll. On college campuses and in the workplace, sexual harassment litigation costs millions of dollars each year. Unless we stop such harassment in our schools and create a consensus early on that this behavior is wrong, our children will pay for this conduct as they grow up.

Bullying: "Intolerable Cruelty"

Bullying, which continues to be part of the school culture, plays out differently for boys and girls. While boys tend to get physical, girls more often bully other girls with verbal assaults that result in excluding another girl or spreading false rumors and gossip about her. Both boys and girls make fun of how others talk and look. A 2001 article, "Bullying," reports that almost 30 percent of teens in the United States are involved in bullying as victims, perpetrators, or both. Same-sex bullying is very common and includes accusing others of being gay or lesbian. Bullying can have a profound impact on how teens feel at school. After repeated gossip about her sexuality appeared in the bathrooms of her school, one high school girl responded, "The experience was awful. I didn't want to go to school. I felt rattled all the time; I felt insecure and vulnerable. School was no longer a safe place for me."

Another high school girl recalled, "When I walked into French class, I saw a paper on my desk and on it was written in bold letters, 'DYKE.' I quickly turned the paper over, slid into my chair, and unsuccessfully tried to hold back my tears. The truth is, I don't know if I'm gay, so I immediately felt exposed, humiliated, and frightened. After school, I told my parents about it, and they suggested that I ignore it. Ignoring it didn't make it stop.

"So I confided in my French teacher after class, and she suggested that I go to the counselor. I resisted at first, because it just seemed like an invitation for more abuse, if anyone else found out about it. The teacher assured me that I could trust the counselor, and she took my situation seriously. She told me that the school had an antibullying policy and there was a procedure for complaints. She was right. After talking to the counselor, I felt less ashamed." If you want to help your child, encourage her to act less like a victim, and act on her behalf if necessary.

"Every day in America . . . 160,000 children miss school for fear of being bullied."

—NATIONAL ASSOCIATION OF SCHOOL PSYCHOLOGISTS

If you find out that your child is the bully, you should be equally concerned. You should explain the seriousness of treating people disrespectfully and have swift consequences for continuing the behavior. You should also support the school's actions when they treat bullying as a serious matter. Excusing or ignoring the behavior encourages it to continue. Bullies often don't really understand how their behavior affects others because their feelings of empathy may be limited. You can help your children by making sure they understand how being targeted by a bully feels and by praising them for more appropriate behavior.

Teens who are targets tend to be more anxious and insecure and will continue to be bullied if they don't know how to stand up for themselves. They may not have the skills to be able to defend themselves. With the indirect way that many girls bully other girls, it happens so fast and insidiously that it's often difficult to track the behavior quickly enough to make it stop. If you learn of any incidents, the best way to stop the viciousness is to teach your daughter how to defend herself and what to say to the bullies. You can teach your daughter the following tips:

* Don't get angry, get funny. Respond with a joke.
* Ignore the bullying; this sends a message that you are not afraid.
* Tell the bullies that you don't like what they are doing; sometimes they may be unaware of their behavior.
* Tell them to stop and leave you alone. Ask your friends to go with you if you don't want to talk to the bullies alone.
* Tell an adult what is happening. It is the adult's responsibility to help stop the bullying.
* Avoid being alone with the bully.

You can also speak to the parents of the bully. The bully's parents may not be aware of their child's behavior or how their own family patterns may be responsible. They may not be as responsive as you would like, but it's one avenue to try. Don't forget to also talk with your child about the harm in remaining an observer or enabler if she knows of or sees bullying taking place. Help her to express disapproval of bullying by not joining in the laughter, teasing, or gossip. Schools can assist by having clear rules and consequences, rather than turning away from bullying incidents and treating the behavior as normal adolescent angst. Demand that schools protect students from a hostile environment.

Girls and Sports: "A Field of Dreams"

Probably no greater culture shift has taken place than in the area of girls' sports. Years ago a girl could only represent her school in uniform as a cheerleader. Today, nearly 2.8 million girls participate in athletics according to the National Collegiate Athletic Association. Implementation of Title IX regulations has made this change possible; without it, the increase in girls' participation in sports would never have happened. We know this because many opponents are still kicking and screaming as resources in schools are distributed more equitably between girls' and boys' sports. With diminishing resources, some of the boys' sports are being cut and others are required to share fields and revise schedules as young women's access to participation opportunities and scholarship dollars increases. Yet there are still too many schools where girls' teams get the most minimal treatment.

Any female athlete will tell you what a positive difference her sport has made in her life. Research has shown that girls who participate in team sports have higher self-esteem and feel better about their bodies. These girls learn how to compete, work as part of a team, and deal with winning and losing, and they are less afraid to take risks. They learn to be efficient and do better academically in school. Girls who are busy with sports have less time for other things that aren't as good for them. Girls who participate in sports are no longer considered to be "tomboys"; outstanding female athletes are beginning to enjoy the preferred status of their male counterparts.

Girls learn life skills, such as citizen advocacy, because of their participation in and love for a sport. Gretchen, a 16-year-old volleyball player, told us how she fought for better athletic facilities for girls when inequities were identified: "When I realized how inferior the girls' facilities were, I got to work. I pulled together my teammates as well as girls from other sports; received support from our parents, coaches, and teachers; and lobbied the school board to fund changes. Although the changes are happening slower than we would like, they are occurring; we're moving in the right direction."

Girls don't consider only Britney Spears or Jessica Simpson to be role models; they are just as likely to admire soccer players Brandi Chastain or Mia Hamm, figure skater Sara Hughes, track star Jackie Joyner-Kersee, basketball player Sheryl Swoopes, or softball player Dot Richardson. As a result of the opportunities and training required by Title IX, we have professional women's basketball leagues and tennis associations. According to Jere Longman in "Women Move Closer to Olympic Equality," during the 2000 Olympics, for the first time, women competed in the same number of team sports as men. Girls and women have proved they have the endurance and talent to excel in sports.

Parents and girls shared wonderful stories about their love of athletics. A 14-year-old girl told us, "Anything that's physically challenging or scary, I know I can accomplish because I never thought I could be a good in-line skater. Once I tried it, I became great!"

One mother told the story of her daughter who didn't do well in school, and the mother worried about her daughter's self-esteem. She said, "I brought Christine to the local swimming pool when she was seven years old. I had to find something that she felt good about. Well, she became the best breaststroker in her age group. She received so much affirmation for her athletic skills. It spilled over into school. Christine became as persistent in school as she was in the swimming pool."

A father of a 15-year-old soccer player reported: "When I first started going to Alicia's games, I had no idea how physical they would be. Nothing stopped these girls from attacking the goal. Her games are every bit as exciting as my son's games. Alicia wants that college scholarship. I have no doubt that she has a real shot."

Another mother said, "Unlike when I was a girl, today I encourage both my son and my daughter to be involved in sports."

Girls' participation in athletics is beginning to pay off in terms of college scholarships. According to Paula Span in "It's a Girl's World," approximately $180 million is spent annually for female athletes. It's less than what is spent on boys' sports, but with one in three girls involved in athletics, the pressure is on for more equitable funding. When evaluating the difference a regulation and advocates can make in the lives of children, consider this: since 1972, female high school and college participation in sports has increased by 847 percent. According to the National Coalition for Women and Girls in Education, "Today 150,916 women compete in intercollegiate sports, accounting for 43 percent of college varsity athletes—an increase of more than 403 percent from 1971." Organizations such as the Women's Sports Foundation, the National Coalition for Women and Girls in Education, and the National Women's Law Center not only track the progress of women's sports but they also lobby, along with other advocates, for more equitable use of resources.

Having strength and fitness as an alternative to wafer-thin bodies is becoming more appealing. We aren't there yet, but there are girls who choose to strive for an athlete's build rather than a model's body. By understanding the benefits of athletics, parents can encourage and support their daughters in their desire to participate in sports and to strive to be fit rather than thin.

Participating in sports doesn't work for everyone, and we don't want to adopt the boys' culture of dismissing nonathletic boys. But today's sports opportunities for girls have allowed them to go beyond playing half-court basketball or being able to demonstrate athleticism only through cheerleading. Sports also help to keep girls in school and off drugs and make them less likely to become pregnant. Holly Bru-

"More girls are coming out for sports, but we need to make sure they're met with the same enthusiasm and institutional support that has accompanied boys all along."

—ISABEL STEWART, Executive Director, Girls Inc.

bach reports in "The Athletic Esthetic," as girls and women "come into their own, [they] have at last begun to feel at home in their bodies, which previously they were only renting. In athletes, we recognize women who own their bodies, inhabiting every inch of them, and the sight of their vitality is exhilarating." Although the playing field is still not level, the possibility of our daughters' realizing their athletic dreams is becoming more and more attainable.

Creating a Positive and Powerful Learning Environment

Girls should feel safe to learn in school, and they should be able to achieve according to their potential without gender limitations. Educators must make sure that curriculum and instructional practices are free from bias; you can hold them to that standard and encourage your daughter by being involved in her education. Parents, teachers, and school administrators alike must intervene when they see disruptive and/or destructive behavior. However, when parents and educators do step in, they must be tuned in to teenage social dynamics, and, for parents, the reality of their daughters' fears and emotions must be considered.

Children—even adolescents—respond positively to high expectations and challenges. You can make it clear that you expect dedication and sustained effort from your daughter in all endeavors. At the same time, avoid putting unnecessary pressure on her by keeping in mind that effort counts, even if accomplishment does not immediately follow. It's beneficial for your daughter to be challenged academically, socially, and athletically. Participating in extracurricular activities is a good way for girls to develop self-confidence, and school should support these expectations.

Some of our daughters may resist participating in extracurricular activities or won't commit to any activity. If you find resistance, explore with your daughter what she is worried about. In many circumstances, it's not the activity but something else that fuels this resistance, such as who is doing the activity and whether your daughter feels she can excel at it. We believe there is something out there for everyone. And it is noteworthy that when girls do participate in extracurricular activities, they assume many of the leadership roles, which enhances their self-confidence. It will benefit your daughter if you help her to identify an interest, skill, or sport in order to increase her spheres of competence. This feeling of competence will make her feel proud. An appreciation of her abilities will increase her self-esteem. A lot of the "noise" can be burned off with physical activity or becoming involved in something she loves to do. Both you and your daughter will benefit from her finding her passion.

6

GIRLS AS FRIENDS

Best Buddies and Friendly Fire

"What do you think are the most important issues/struggles facing teenage girls today? The need to belong. Many girls feel that they don't belong anywhere or with anyone, so they begin to act insensibly and thus run into trouble. Many girls will do anything so they can be 'cool' and belong to a group. For example, some may try drugs so their 'friends' will like them."

—From a 15-year-old's summit questionnaire in
Pamela Haag's "Fitting In, Voices of a Generation:
Teenage Girls on Sex, School, and Self"

When sitting with a group of girls, we were struck by the hum that constantly surrounds them. There is so much energy, like the rustle of butterflies or the splendor of lightning bugs, moving all the time. Female friendship can offer girls a tremendous opportunity to experience invaluable companionship, support, and joy. Friendships between girls can incorporate the positive qualities of loyalty, trust, and collaboration. These are the friendships that sustain us. Many of us have friendships that we can trace back to elementary school. We can move cross-country and not talk to one another for several months, but when we meet again, it is as if we saw each other just a minute ago.

Common experiences among friends are priceless, and girls are capable of creating nurturing and loving friendships. We saw these kinds of friendships when meeting with our focus groups. One group of ninth graders had been together in a mother-daughter book group since they were in second grade. Some went to different high schools, but the connection among them, the respect they felt for one another, was evident. Other girls we met with also had their "heart girls."

Michele, 16 years old, said, "I count on my friends for everything. I have one friend whose parents recently split up, and I was talking to her about how she felt. She said her parents wanted her to go and see a therapist, and she told them, 'If I can't say these things to my friends, then how can I say them to a therapist?' That made me think about how important our friends really are at this age." A parent of a high school junior described her daughter's group as "a very welcoming, gentle, nurturing group of friends. Their friendships don't conform to the nasty things we read about. I feel the girls take good care of each other."

Maggie, 15 years old, said, "I know there are girls who are mean to each other. They say they're friends, and they act like they're friends when they're with each other, but they always talk behind each other's backs. My friends are over that now. We support and comfort each other; we are really just there for our friends." Maggie's mother confirms this observation: "Maggie's friends are supportive of each other. I hear on the phone, 'Oh, look, you can do this. What you have to do is . . .' I tell Maggie how important it is to be straight with your friends, but more significantly, I try to model how to be a good friend." Positive connections and friendships are what get us through life.

Boys and Girls as Friends

Friendships with boys have a special function for many girls. Matt, 17, said, "Girls have an easier time being friends to boys because they are satisfied with being friends without the sexual component. I think that we aren't as critical as girls, and we see things from a different point of view. My best 'girl' friend, Tara, usually calls me to see if she is overreacting to something her boyfriend, Justin, said or did. Social stuff is not as dramatic for us, and we can be helpful by offering a different perspective."

Maggie, a high school junior, said, "Thank God for Sam. I asked him to so many sweet 16s and Sadie Hawkins dances; he's my default date. We're just friends, but I count on his friendship and unconditional support. When he's standing with a group of guys, I never have to feel uncomfortable about joining them. When I walk up to the group, Sam puts his arm around me and welcomes me with the sweetest hello. I've cried on his shoulder and listened to fears that he tells no one else." A friendship with a boy can function as a break for girls. Besides offering trust and intimacy without judgment, it gives girls insight into how boys approach the world.

Cliques: Approach with Caution

Friendships are key to how girls feel, but they can have a dark side during these years. Fourteen-year-old Ashley said, "My friends are my life." Cynthia, a high school senior, said, "Nothing is worse than a friend's betrayal." Another girl reported, "My worst fear is being alone." Trying to be a part of a group, to fit in, is one of the tasks of adolescent life. Ask any girl and she can describe in detail who belongs to the "in" group, although she may not be able to verbalize precisely what makes them "cool."

"Teen cliques are more fluid than adults think, but each has its own distinc-
tive tribal markings, from hippy chic to body art to buttoned-down prep."
—SHARON BEGLEY, "A World of Their Own"

For every girl there is a challenge, whether it's to get into the "cool"
group, to stay in the "cool" group, or to decide to stay out of the mostly
revolving-door cycle of teen group life. For most girls, middle school
is the transition between what were solid friendships in elementary
school and the chaotic nature of friendships during adolescence. Making this transition is one of the greatest challenges for parents and their
daughters. Parents—mothers especially—approach seventh and eighth
grade with trepidation, because all of us remember what these middle
school years were like.

Social groups or cliques tend to be based on common interests
and activities, race and ethnicity, and socioeconomic class. They can
be fluid, but there are usually some permanent members who, as one
15-year-old observed about the "cool" group, "always look just right."
These groups can be identified by the labels they wear, the sports they
play, their school activities, whether they take drugs, and how social
and "fast" they are. "In my school," Joanna, 15, reported, "If you wear
Abercrombie or Old Navy, you're a nerd, a preppie. They can also be
smart, but they aren't the cool kids." The rules are often very specific
and differ from school to school. What is cool in the city of Denver is
probably different from what is cool in the suburbs of Los Angeles.

Parents and girls alike struggle with trying to figure out why certain girls are more popular than others. In reviewing *Thirteen*, a movie
about two teenage girls' obsession with popularity, Stephen Hunter
concludes, "Cool, really, is an ideal, invented by the media, against
which we judge ourselves and against which we find ourselves wanting, always, no matter what. There are seven naturally cool people in

the world, and all of them are fighter pilots with multiple victories, and they all know that if they talk about being cool, then they aren't cool anymore. You can't want it; you have to be it."

One mother related the following conversation she had with her teenage daughter. Eleanor said, "I kept saying to Rebecca, 'What is it about this group that I keep hearing about? Are they smarter? Do they get better grades? Are they richer? Do they have bigger houses? What is it that identifies them?' Rebecca kept saying, 'No, it's not that. It's not that.' She finally said, 'I think it's just that they assume that they are popular and they're entitled to belong to this group, and the rest of us will go our merry way and make our friends elsewhere. They think they are in this golden bubble. I call them glossy girls.'" "Glossy girls" are not easily defined, but everyone knows who "they" are, even parents and teachers.

We have discussed backstabbing, gossiping, and bullying as part of girl culture. Adolescent girls, says Kathleen Vail in "How Girls Hurt," "live in a world where best friends can become enemies overnight, where one look from another girl can mean the difference between isolation and belonging. It's a world where no one tells you why you can no longer sit at the lunch table with your friends, where secrets are traded like currency."

Middle School Is the Worst

In middle school, the wide variation in emotional and physical maturity exacerbates what is already the complex process of development. This is a time of constant emotional upheaval where long-standing friendships can blow up in an instant. Middle school is also the beginning of interest-based friendships, an additional source of change and adjustment.

Jenny said, "When I was in seventh grade, I looked like I was 10 years old. I was straight all over and could practically fit a bracelet on my thigh! My best friend, Chloe, acted like a girl in high school and had the body of a woman. We made a funny pair. For a year or so, we had few interests in common, and I felt left out of her new group. It was lonely and tough, but I wasn't interested in hanging out and flirting with boys. I was barely finished watching Nickelodeon. Eventually, I, too, grew, but the friendship was different. I found other friends in the meantime, but it wasn't easy, and I missed Chloe."

Girls develop physically and emotionally at such different rates that, as one mother described her daughter's friends, "One friend of Sarah still looks like a little girl, and another looks like she could be birthing babies." The hormones kick in, and when they do, some girls are more socially sophisticated than others, become boy crazy sooner, and are less interested in their friends who are not primping and grooming and hanging out at the mall.

Jenny's and Sarah's experiences are universal because the range of development in 12- to 14-year-old girls is so diverse and so public. These differences complicate friendships for girls because what they once had in common no longer exists; they are literally at different life stages. For example, Darcy, mother of 13-year-old Ellen, said, "Some of the girls are ready for girl-boy parties. For my daughter, she is only ready to flirt with flirting by instant messaging boys. If girls aren't ready for boy-girl parties, they usually aren't in the popular group. Ellen wasn't being called for sleepovers anymore because she wasn't ready for boys, and her former friends 'didn't want a baby around.'"

Elizabeth, mother of 14-year-old Katie, had a similar experience: "For my daughter, middle school was a series of losses. She lost friends because she wasn't as precocious as some of her elementary school friends. They wouldn't speak to her and actually told her she wasn't welcome in their group any longer. Katie lost confidence in herself and spent a lot of time alone watching TV and reading. It was incredibly painful for me to watch. Although it was painful for Katie, I'm not sure she didn't survive it better than I did. Once she got to high school, there were so many more choices of activities where she could meet new kids."

High School: The Changing Landscape

Friendships do change during the high school years. There are more options and greater opportunities for autonomy and interest-based relationships. The girls in our focus groups agreed that as long as they have a stable group of friends, they are comfortable in high school. Brooke, a 14-year-old high school freshman, said, "It's OK to be in a loser clique in high school; it's harder in middle school because you are more noticeable."

Recently, troubled-girl books have painted a dismal picture of teenage female culture. We often hear about and see images of the tall, shapely blond at the center of the social hub who uses her good looks and popularity to attract or marginalize other "ordinary" females. These "queen bees" or "alpha girls," as Rosalind Wiseman refers to them in *Queen Bees and Wannabes* and as seen in the movie, *Mean Girls*, are the "cool" cutthroat girls who value their social omnipotence over friendship, solidarity, and compassion. Then there are the "wanna-bes," the "betas," who will follow any given formula to gain the good graces of the queen bees. In addition, as Susannah Meadows tells us in "Meet the Gamma Girls," Laura Sessions Stepp gives us a third, more resilient group of females: the "gammas." These are the girls we don't hear much about. In a 2003 interview, Laura Stepp shared with us a wonderful story about her "gamma girls":

> I invented the phrase, "gamma girls," because I saw a lot of girls who didn't fit the alpha mold, the old-fashioned, manipulative, teasing bitch. There are a lot of girls who are very strong, who are not that way, and maybe there isn't a word for them. So that's when I literally went to the dictionary and started looking up alpha, beta, gamma, trying to figure out what we would call these girls so they would have something to aim toward that was not a typical alpha. I also wanted to figure out a category that we could frame in a pos-

itive way so that it was something that girls could be proud of. Actually, this is so cool. After Susannah Meadows's article in *Newsweek* came out in June 2002, I was riding down to the beach. I saw these two bands, and they had written in white soap on the windows of their car, 'We are gamma girls.' I found that the new term gave them a sense of empowerment, that they could be assertive, without being a "queen bee" or "wannabe."

The "gammas" may be the more average-looking, studious, kind, compassionate, and free-spirited girls who feel comfortable in their own skin and don't feel it's necessary to put someone else down to enhance their social stature. This independence may stem from being picked on or standing on the outskirts of popularity in elementary or middle school. Feelings of not belonging at a crucial time of social development may have driven these girls to define molds of their own design. Meadows adds that these girls "don't long to be invited to parties—they're too busy writing an opinion column in the school newspaper, horseback riding," or reading or spending time with family members or religious groups to get caught up in the need to be or appear to be socially savvy.

By following a self-designed path on the outskirts of the group, these girls develop insight and maturity beyond that typically found among their more group-dependent peers. Their experience with groups is more fluid: they have the ability to move in and out of groups at their own initiative. Unlike the popular girls, who seem to have the greatest pressure to grow up quickly, "gamma" girls often have the self-confidence and self-respect that allow them to escape the peer group pressure to experiment with drugs and early sexual activity.

Some girls choose not to get caught up in what can be a vicious cycle of instant inclusion and exclusion. These girls may share three or four best friends and treat everyone else, as one girl described, as "an associate." Not depending on a particular social group allows girls to explore interests and develop skills and avoid being boxed in by a particular set of norms and standards.

One mother of a 16-year-old girl described her daughter this way: "Jasmine keeps it simple. She doesn't aspire to be in any group, but you can always find her with one of her four best friends. I have taught her that only she is important to her development and state of mind. I want her to be who she is, not what others want her to be. Other than me, Jasmine knows that nobody can take better care of her than she can. She has to learn to take care of herself, not at the expense of others, but to learn to trust herself."

Girls who are always trying to be popular often do not get the opportunity to think independently. Even for those girls who always "dress the right way," the challenge to maintain this status can be limiting. Parents who have chosen not to push or fixate on their child's popularity can take comfort in knowing that there are benefits to not belonging to the "cool" group.

My Daughter, Not Myself

During these years, you should try to use, as much as possible, detached engagement and avoid reliving your own experiences through your daughter. This does not discount the value of sharing common experiences. Seventeen-year-old Nadia said, "I remember telling my mother that I was the flattest girl in my grade and was worried about not having my period yet. My mother smiled and said, 'Don't worry, Nadia, in our family we don't develop until we're 16. Your time will come.' I didn't know how she knew what she knew, but it made me feel normal, so I felt better."

Nadia's mother gave her the information that fostered the insight necessary to normalize her experience of late development. As valuable as these insights are, you have to be cautious in comparing your own experiences in light of current teenage life. To be successful, it's best to be present in your daughter's life and base your advice and support on *her* experience. In addition, you can be more effective if you don't allow yourself to become overly involved or invested in your daughter's popularity and social status.

Whatever group she belongs to, when our daughters get hurt, there is nothing worse. Almost nothing brings out our protective instinct like our children being bullied or excluded. Being left out can affect a girl's achievement in school and her sense of self-worth. Some 40 years later, mothers can remember girls who had power when they were in school. Linda, mother of 14-year-old Renee, said, "When my daughter is sad, it is so painful to watch. I know I bring my own baggage to the situation. No one that I know would ever want to go back to being a 13- or 14-year-old girl."

In addition, unfortunately, as Rosalind Wiseman observes in the article "How Girls Hurt" published by Kathleen Vail, a lot of this negative behavior stays under the radar of teachers and parents. In schools, because this covert aggression does not disrupt the classroom and is not physical, the behavior is often ignored. Wiseman believes, "Women want to ignore it, either because it brings back painful memories of their own childhood relationships or because they think calling attention to it makes women look bad. For these reasons it's hard to see the actions as bullying."

As long as people tolerate or encourage this kind of passive-aggressive behavior, it will continue. Parents in our focus group shared stories of parents who, as one mother described, "support the pecking order. They are happy if their daughter has cool friends, designer clothes, and a custom-plated cell phone. It's almost as if they are cool if their kids are in a cool group." Girls will not be tormented as frequently if parents emphasize to their daughters that exclusion and bullying are not acceptable behaviors and remind them how it feels to be rejected. Schools also must call students on this behavior. The culture has to change, but without an intentional effort by parents and other adult role models, this behavior will persist.

In the meantime, you should teach your daughter not only that you won't tolerate bullying but also how to deal with conflict and disappointment and affirm her ability to make new friends. One mother told the story of how important it is to pay close attention to the emotions of our daughters rather than our own emotions. Charlotte said, "My daughter changed schools and friends from middle to high school. She is introverted, and when her old friends stopped calling, I was sick about it. She didn't call them, and I couldn't see beyond that old group.

"I missed the part that she was making new friends in her new school and was perfectly content. Once I got that, I put a positive spin on her present experience, that things were OK because she had new friends to be with." Parents must support their daughters in exploring other friendships and stress the importance of being around girls who make them feel good about themselves, who are trustworthy and loyal. These are friends whose friendship will benefit girls throughout their lives.

Missed-Fit: The Outsider

Your daughter may be an individual, one who marches to her own drum. As one parent described, "The world looks real different, and the way other kids respond to her is very different." Not fitting into the culture of middle and high school can be a difficult and painful experience for many teens. The experience doesn't have to be all bad, but being on the outside does present challenges. The biggest challenge for teenage girls is the message they receive that they are not acceptable the way they are.

These girls can look different, have different interests, or have a different sexual orientation. Girls can also look like other girls and act like other girls but feel different from most of the girls around them. Lily, 14, said, "When I'm with certain people I'm not that comfortable with and try to make conversation, I'm really fake because I'm trying to be like them. I don't have much in common with them, and I have to think of things to say. I can usually come up with something to say, but I don't like the way I feel when I have to pretend."

Girls who don't fit in suffer. Peer groups can torment girls through indirect aggression and exclusion. You can't fully protect your daughter from this cruelty and rejection; however, you can help to create opportunities for her to develop success in other spheres. You can assess whether your daughter seems different because she *is* different or if she acts different because she is protecting herself from feeling like an outsider.

Even if your daughter looks and acts the part of a girl who fits in, sometimes you have to look deeper, because she may not feel that she fits in. This is where your self-awareness can make a difference for your daughter and, ultimately, how she defines herself. Stacey, a 52-year-old mother, said, "I never thought of myself as not fitting in. I was a cheerleader in high school, was popular, and got good grades, but some things bored me that other girls enjoyed. I had more interest in carpentry than cooking and have always noted that if you knit, sew, and build but don't cook, other women always comment on your lack of skills."

As psychologist Dr. Susan Mikesell says, "If you can pass as a successful girl, your feelings of being an outsider might be hidden, even from yourself." Stacey continued: "Because I have had so little interest in traditional women's tasks, I've labeled myself as lazy, a tag I've carried for a very long time. Only recently have I learned that I wasn't lazy, I was just different. Now I appreciate my skills in a nonpejorative way.

"I wish my mother could have helped me to appreciate my own talents, but how could she? She was a product of her generation. She could play golf like a pro and build furniture, but her lack of ability in the kitchen, including her vast collection of frozen dinners, was the subject of many family jokes. With my own daughter, I feel I have an opportunity not only to give her permission to stretch out of the boundaries of what 'traditional' women have an interest in and are supposed to be good at, but not to judge herself negatively if she doesn't choose to excel in traditional women's roles and work."

Women don't have to do it all, we just have to be in charge of what we choose to do and not be made to feel embarrassed or ashamed if we are different. Because of this belief, we coined the term, "missed-fit," rather than misfit, because misfit is a projection of someone else's standards and carries a negative judgment. You must try to be sensitive when choosing words to describe differences and must avoid harmful judgment.

The danger for girls who don't feel that they fit in is in developing a self-concept in opposition to what is considered normal behavior, a process similar to what girls of color do in opposition to mainstream culture. Sixteen-year-old Emma, dressed in black from head to toe with shoe-polish hair, combat boots, and blood-red lipstick, said, "I'm not one of those petite, squeaky clean, kiss-ass girlie girls. This is who I am, like it or leave it." Her mother, Barbara, said, "Really, who is Emma? Is she Goth because she doesn't fit in, or doesn't she fit in because she is Goth? I'm not clear and worry that Emma has created this persona in her own defense.

"Emma's way of rebelling forces her to the opposite side of the spectrum. I just want her to know who she is, because being Goth gives her the false illusion of choosing whether she is in the popular group or not. Emma's defense is that she thinks she has rejected the popular kids, and I'm not sure she really believes that. She has chosen an extreme persona, and, really, Emma just wants to feel like she's the one in control."

Many girls become frustrated and angry when their parents, peers, or society do not support them the way they are. Ali, now 15 years old, was happy with who she was until her friends started to exclude her in middle school. When she would go to the mall with certain friends, she could tell that they were ashamed to be seen with her, because these friends had joined the "girlie" pack. Friends would tell Ali to pretend she didn't know them if they ran into other girls from school.

At 13, Ali was feeling so ostracized by others that she couldn't stomach the image of Barbie. Barbie represented all that she was not: tall, busty, and thin. Weight was an issue for Ali, as was looking a certain way so she would fit in. One day she set Barbie on fire on the front lawn of her house. Ali called attention to herself by doing extreme things. She saw herself as the "weird girl" and acted out the role with real flamboyance. Her relationship with her parents became strained. They had not been supportive of her individual traits and strengths throughout her childhood, and, in their effort to tell her to try to fit in and "act normal," they had given her a strong message that she was not normal and was a disappointment to them. This only reinforced her extreme behavior and her belief that she was odd. Their expectations created a self-fulfilling prophecy.

As a result, Ali didn't have a secure sense of herself, which caused her to establish new relationships too quickly with people who ultimately disappointed her. Her identity was built around calling attention to herself by saying things such as, "You remember me, and I'm the weirdo, the one who threw herself on the gym floor at the school dance." The label "weirdo" had given her an identity and entitled her to act out. Unfortunately, because of this behavior, she felt estranged rather than empowered.

Ali felt so alienated that she pulled away from her parents. Things got so bad that they sent her to a wilderness program to straighten her out, which turned out to be a positive experience. At the camp Ali lost weight, and her appearance became more pleasing to others. Her parents were happy and told her how good she looked. So why isn't this a slam-dunk success story?

Losing weight and changing one's appearance creates its own dilemma. Ali's mom was proud of her changes and praised her. Ali was getting the message that she was more acceptable. The dilemma was that she felt better and looked good, but only because she fit into the mold she fought so hard to reject. This change left Ali feeing confused and insecure.

Ali's parents were so relieved to see their daughter fit in that they didn't appreciate her need to develop an identity as someone other than the "weird girl" who had lost weight. This change would have been an easier transition if her parents had validated her discomfort with this new acceptance. Ali was mad that people were accepting her for no other reason than that she fit into a more traditional mold. She still felt unknown to others.

With appropriate help, Ali can build an inner core and present herself in an authentic way, rather than in opposition to other girls (because she didn't fit in). Ali needs to value and continue to work on the real qualities that she possesses and to verbalize her hurt. Ali's parents could benefit from professional guidance for added support.

This anecdote is an example of how much more difficult the passage to adulthood is when parents, in spite of commitment to their children and desire to see them be happy, do not give them the validation they need the most. In many instances, parents may not have the skills needed to help their daughter. If you find yourself struggling with the problems that interfere with your daughter's happiness and ability to belong, it is important to get help. This guidance may be as simple as seeking counseling or parenting education information or talking with friends you think have wisdom to share.

Your job is to teach your daughter the value of who she is and to highlight what is special about her. A girl who learns to like herself because of who she is has a much better chance of attracting friends. Having a few soul mates is all any of us needs. Every girl has talents and unique qualities; if you recognize these traits in your daughter, you can help her to feel good about herself. Much of teenage conduct is really a search for self. Even if a girl struggles in her peer group, she can get through this period with appropriate parental and other adult support.

Janice, a traditional mother, shared the story of her daughter, who was an edgy teenager. Their differences created a potentially lethal combination. Liza dyed her hair red and kelly green and had multiple piercings. At first, her mother thought that she would not survive this period, because Liza seemed so foreign. But with help from friends and a therapist, Janice learned to appreciate that her daughter was a good writer, did community service, and was respectful. Once Liza's parents acknowledged these positive traits, they were able to give her validation, which, in turn, allowed Liza to use her independence in a positive way. Janice survived, and Liza thrived.

Janice said, "I look at Liza with awe. After Liza dropped out of college, she had to pay for the credits she missed. Liza moved back home in order to make enough money to get an apartment. Once she had a steady job, she moved out and went back to college part-time. Liza just graduated college at 25. I have no doubts that she can take care of herself, and by the way, her hair is back to its original color." Janice's story demonstrates that by supporting your daughter, regardless of how different she is from you, you can help her develop into a competent and self-confident adult.

Sexual Orientation: Maintaining a Balanced Perspective

Confusion about one's sexual identity is not uncommon during adolescence. In fact, "approximately 40 percent of our daughters experience sexual feelings toward another girl at least once during their adolescent or teen years, and this doesn't mean they will be lesbians," says Lynn Ponton in "Mind and Body: If She Thinks She's a Lesbian." Girls who realize that they are lesbians often are aware early on that they don't fit in and they are not sure why.

Despite increased awareness of and media attention on lesbians, homosexual teenagers continue to face many challenges, which include feeling different from peers, feeling guilty about their sexual orienta-

"I think we are doing some things better than teens that came before us. We are trying to more honestly face sexism, racism, and homophobia. My friends and I have many deep conversations about these kinds of issues. Last year two girls came together to the senior prom and it was no big deal."

—High school–age focus group participant

tion, worrying about their parents' response, and being rejected and harassed by others. The fear of rejection from both society and parents is so strong that keeping the secret can be fatal. Lesbian teens exhibit signs of depression, manifested by isolating themselves socially and finding it hard to concentrate. These signs of distress should not be ignored, because gay and lesbian youth are two to six times more likely to attempt suicide than straight teens. According to the American Academy of Child and Adolescent Psychiatry's website, they account for 30 percent of all completed suicides among teens. Gay and lesbian teens who do have the courage to "come out" risk being teased mercilessly.

A lesbian teen told us, "Going through the halls, I'd get called names and pushed. There was never any end to people laughing at me. Some of the girls wouldn't be friends with me because they thought I would always be coming on to them. Do they come on to every boy? I don't think so. Why wouldn't I want to be just friends like everyone else?" With this response to their sexual orientation, lesbian and gay teens are forced into isolation at a time when they need connection and support.

Most parents have a difficult time accepting their daughter as a lesbian. Ponton states, "Parents neither cause their daughters to become lesbians, nor can they change the reality." Amanda, 18, reported, "I went through hell because there was no one for me to talk to. I had these feelings, and I couldn't explain them . . . but they hurt, and I needed someone to talk to. I never got that, and I needed it." If your daughter identifies herself as a lesbian, you must listen to her with respect and avoid dismissing her by saying that she's going through a temporary phase. Support is available for parents who feel confused, angry, or unhappy about their daughter's sexual orientation. Groups such as Parents, Family and Friends of Lesbians and Gays (PFLAG), whose contact information is available on the Internet, can provide you with the support of other parents who will share their own experiences and wisdom.

Integration of a positive adult identity is a challenge for both lesbian and gay teenagers because they learn from a young age that being gay carries a stigma. Lauren, a high school junior, said, "I have a hard time around my girlfriends because they often say things about queers, fags, and dykes, and it cuts through me like a knife. I haven't told anyone at school that I'm a lesbian, because I'm just not ready. And the more offhand comments I hear, the less secure I get. It's starting to get in the way of my relationships, and I find myself being alone more. It's simpler to stay away than to listen to all the insensitive comments and judgments that make me feel worthless.

"This summer I worked at a day camp with a counselor who started a support group for lesbians at her school. I wish I had a group of friends that I could be real with. Maybe it would make me feel secure enough to open up to my straight friends." Life for lesbian teenagers is even more difficult than for other teenage girls, so their need for their parents' help and support is even greater.

Lauren's friend at camp is one of many teenagers who do not shy away from the subject of homosexuality. According to Jesse Green's article "Out and Organized," many brave teens are part of an emerging gay youth agenda that addresses safe schools, suicide prevention, and AIDS prevention. Other lesbian teens are taking their girlfriend to the prom and refusing to hide their preference from other teenagers.

Homophobia is still powerful in American society. Even with the recent Supreme Court decision *Lawrence & Garner v. Texas* and the proliferation of gay-themed television shows and increased visibility of noted homosexuals in the media, it is still a struggle to be different.

When you talk to your daughter about homophobia, it is important to discuss how this bias is used to keep people confined to rigid sex roles that prevent our girls and boys from being themselves.

"... One Is Silver and the Other Gold"

Connection is critical for keeping people mentally and physically healthy. Friendships enrich the quality of our lives, but enduring and

---

FRIEND INVENTORY

These are questions to start a conversation with your daughter about friendship. What you learn will give you insight into her world. Don't put her on the spot by asking all of the questions at once. Wait for an opportunity when the subject comes up or seems right, and let the conversation flow. This can happen over several different conversations.

1. What do you think a friend is? What words come to mind? Can you think of three words to describe a good friend?
2. What are the different groups of kids in your school?
3. Where do you fit in? Do you see yourself as a member of one group, or can you move among groups?
4. Is there a group that you would like to be a part of but aren't? How does it make you feel?
5. If you are in a group, do you know of kids who are excluded who would like to be part of your group?
6. How do you tell a friend if you are mad at her or him?
7. Do you have boys as friends? Are there things you would tell boys that you wouldn't tell your girlfriends?
8. How would your friends describe you?

---

authentic friendships take work. From those that are worth the investment, girls can learn the value of staying in a relationship that works for them. But not every friend is worth the investment—a difficult but valuable life lesson.

We want our daughters to become authentic adults; this process begins when they are children. Authentic friends give you permission to be yourself. They allow for disagreements and differences and avoid feelings of shame when a girl has complicated and confusing thoughts. When girls know who they are and accept themselves, they can avoid making risky decisions under social pressure. They can also make and keep friends who will stay connected to them, even after disagreements and disappointments. You can model for your daughter how to build and sustain positive friendships.

One of the best strategies is to get to know the parents of your daughter's friends. This tells your daughter that you care about what she does and are interested in who her friends are. It's also important to support friendships between boys and girls and not assume there is necessarily a sexual component. You can validate for your daughter the qualities that create friendships and bring out the best in her by helping her to develop a strong sense of self, which is crucial for her to create and maintain positive teenage friendships. When she has confidence in her abilities, can take personal responsibility for her own behavior, and can empathize with others, she has the components she needs to be a good friend and to better protect herself from the insensitivity of others.

Cutting Through
the Chatter and
Finding Connection

PARENTING

What's Love Got to Do with It?

"I think that parenting has been like a staircase, and I've had to learn how to be a mother at each new step as my daughter changes. I remember thinking when she was two, 'Oh, I've got this down.' And as soon as I felt I was on secure ground, she was different, and I had to learn to be different, too. I'm actually more comfortable now that she is a teenager. I feel really attuned to her. I feel like we vibrate like a string, like I really understand her. I know that some of this is wishful thinking, but I enjoy this feeling. Within the last year or two of adolescence, I noticed a clear separation on her part. So once again, I'm coming to grips with the realization that I have to back up a little and let her grow. I'm aware that we are moving to the next step and hoping that the closeness will come back again if her dad and I let her have some space."

—Focus group parent

A s parents, you may often underestimate the importance of your role during the teenage years. Part of being a teenager is to begin to separate from one's parents and become more independent. It is normal for children to become more critical and more assertive about their opinions during this period. Parents often misinterpret this as an indicator that they should be less involved in their children's lives. Girls' relationships with their parents are generally fraught with so much conflict that moms and dads may want to withdraw and become less engaged out of frustration and weariness.

Even though your daughter begs for her own space and disappears into her bedroom cocoon to talk with her girlfriends, she still wants contact with you. On the surface, her disappearance makes it easy to assume your daughter is no longer interested in maintaining the same connection with you that she had when she was a snuggly preteen, but the truth is, you're still her most important support system. Even though teenage girls are struggling with how to gain autonomy—typically expressed as, "Mom, all right already, get out of my business and leave me alone"—they really need more, not less, adult support and guidance. They need information and strategies to cope with issues pertaining to friendships, school, boys, and sexuality. Girls approach these issues by asking such questions as, How can I say no to a boy without hurting his feelings? Can I call a boy if he hasn't called me? What can I say to my friend who was talking behind my back? To be effective, your guidance must be presented in a supportive, nonjudgmental way. This support requires a real balancing act.

Because so many conversations start out calmly and end in anger, tears, defiance, and back talk, many parents become discouraged and fail to reconnect with their daughter after a meltdown. Parents are also unsure about how to comfort and talk to teenagers without starting the adversarial cycle all over again.

Jenna, a high school senior, recounted, "Dinner at my house usually began with polite conversation and civility. A few minutes into the meal my parents would inevitably ask a question that felt like prying, and I would answer them with attitude. Then they would give me a look of displeasure, and I would respond with loathing and disgust. Many nights followed this pattern. My parents would ask me questions such as, 'Who are you going to see tonight?' and I would answer, 'My friends.' Then they would say, 'Which friends?' and on and on and on, until I would finally leave the house angry. They could never be happy with the information I gave them. It never seemed to satisfy their needs."

Deborah, the mother of 14-year-old Lucy, remembered saying, "'Lucy, don't forget to call Grandma to thank her for your birthday present.' Lucy shrieked, 'Mom, you've reminded me three times this week about calling Grandma. Let it go already! You don't think I'm responsible, so you bug me about the same things over and over again.' Before I could utter a word in my defense, Lucy continued to lash out angrily that she was perfectly capable of remembering to call her grandma. It's amazing how quickly an innocent interaction ignites into a full-scale war."

By comparison, child rearing in the early years is a walk in the park. It feels so easy to protect younger children. It's easy to make them happy when we can just take them to McDonald's and buy them a Happy Meal. One father lamented, "I just want to wrap her in cellophane until she reaches 25." Another parent wistfully suggested, "I'm no longer under the illusion that I have ultimate control. I lost it as my daughter got older; she beat it out of me." Yet another said, "I'd like to sleep for a few years and wake up when adolescence is over. The thought of my daughter dating, driving, and drinking fills me with terror."

Conventional wisdom is that it's harder to raise daughters than it is sons because daughters have so much angst and drama in their lives. We disagree. We may think that it's easier to raise sons, but, in fact, their issues are just as loaded. It's simply hard to raise teenagers. However, the expectations parents and society may have about girls' adolescence and boys' adolescence can be very different. Society values protecting daughters by keeping them close. In contrast, society encourages parents to help boys become men by pushing them away so they can resolve issues on their own. These sex-role expectations influence parenting throughout childhood and create a lifetime of interactions based on whether your child is a boy or a girl. These interactions influence the way your daughter feels about herself and relates to the world.

Gender strongly influences the relationships that many parents have with their children. Parents tolerate more distance from sons than we think is healthy, and the opposite may be true for daughters. Parents are often overly invested in the minute details of girls' lives when what we need to do is to give them some space. We tend to give our sons more slack and don't expect them to plug into family events and outings as much as we do our daughters. In a sense, we count our sons out when we should count them in, while we should consider giving our daughters a bit more freedom.

Relationships are emotionally charged in different ways for moms and for dads. For mothers, raising teenage daughters is like going back to the future, watching themselves while watching their daughters and reminding moms of experiences they had as young girls. While this identification with their own teenage years can provide mothers with greater empathy, understanding, and guidance, it can also resurrect childhood pain and cause moms to have knee-jerk reactions. For these reasons, some mothers may have a harder time with their daughters during the teenage years.

Allen, the father of Kelly, confirmed this difference: "Kelly doesn't jump down my throat like she does her mother's. She even laughs at my bad jokes and isn't on edge, ready to pounce on my every word like she does her mother's. I have more leeway than my wife to deliver tough messages with much less back talk from Kelly." Mothers and daughters, like fathers and sons, often wrestle with separating their personal experiences.

Often, fathers and daughters seem to have fewer everyday problems. They argue about safety and achievement issues, but the relationship may be less stormy because fathers have a built-in ability to differentiate and separate from their daughters. Unlike with their moms, girls don't share the same familiar buttons. With unconditional love, this type of connection with dads promotes an autonomy that is healthy for girls.

David, the father of 13-year-old Ashley, said, "Ashley is less critical of my appearance than [of] her mom's. She is her mom's fashion police, scrutinizing and critiquing her mother's shoes and clothes. Happily, I am free of the same judgment. If I wear something goofy, she laughs and says, 'Isn't my daddy cute?' Ashley is much more forgiving with me, and I am more relaxed with her."

On the other hand, parenting teenage girls may also be more difficult for a father because, never having been a girl, he lacks an understanding of the context of his daughter's life. His daughter's experiences are less familiar to him. For example, girls may engage in relationship issues that seem simple to dads, whereas for girls, these struggles may be more complicated. This lack of experience or insight may also lead to a tumultuous relationship between fathers and daughters.

Self-awareness is an invaluable tool in parenting. Research by Daniel Siegel and Mary Hartzell, published in *Parenting from the Inside Out*, shows that the best predictor of a child's security of attachment is how parents make sense of their own lives. There is benefit to having an accurate understanding of where you come from and who you are. With this understanding, it is possible for parents to enhance their personal relationships and be more successful in guiding their children through each developmental stage.

Mothers and Daughters: Here, There, and Everywhere

When you listen to your daughter, hear her desire to be independent and different from you. Understand your daughter's fear that she'll become too much like you, while at the same time she's afraid that she'll lose your love if she doesn't. Our culture teaches us that to be too close means to be symbiotic and enmeshed. This makes it difficult to view attachment and connection in a positive light. The following metaphor may further explain healthy attachment versus an enmeshed relationship. Healthy attachment is like scuba diving with a buddy. Together, the divers can enjoy the underwater sights, checking in with each other to make sure they are OK. Being enmeshed would mean that the divers share a tank of air, each needing the other to breathe.

The subtext of many arguments between mothers and daughters during adolescence concerns attachment and affiliation, including such questions as How close is too close? and How far is too far? Mothers and daughters should strive for autonomy *and* connectedness. Finding this balance is a high-wire act. It's a mother's job to support her daughter's independence without disconnecting, a situation that inevitably creates confusion and tension. Women understand their historical caretaking role in the family, but this role is often inconsistent with encouraging autonomy for their daughters.

The bond between mother and daughter is far more powerful than most of us realize. This bond is particularly strong during adolescence, a period that offers an opportunity for both mothers and daughters to discover and rediscover their identities. Nancy Snyderman reports in *Girl in the Mirror* that the "past, present, and future collide when we look into our daughters' faces. All of our dreams— those we've realized and those we consider beyond our grasp—are in the room with us."

Because of their powerful interconnection, women have complex relationships with their daughters. As one mother said, "It's like a mixture of oil and water. I'm always on the verge of an argument—something not pretty could happen at any moment. I always feel that I'm dancing on glass and could slip." The relationship between mother and daughter is primordial, setting the stage for all other relationships in a girl's life. It vitally contributes to her resilience by providing a foundation for healthy development. The mother-daughter relationship also

"A mother stands in a room with a mirror on each side. One mirror holds the reflection of her own mother, and in the other she sees a reflection of her daughter."

—Focus group parent

protects our daughters by giving them a greater ability to cope with adversity.

In *Motherless Daughter*, Hope Edelman states that our own mothers are our most direct connection to our past. They set examples for us by their actions and inactions, by their strengths and weaknesses. Our relationships with our mothers inform us about our relationships with our daughters. Nancy Snyderman also writes, "For every girl who makes the journey from child to woman, the first mirror in which she looks is the mirror of her mother's face. . . . In the room with us are our past selves, the adolescent girls we once were. Our own mothers' words echo when we talk."

As the mother of a daughter, you inhabit two roles at the same time: the past role of daughter, which may not end until after your own mother's death, and the role as mother of your own daughter. In a sense, you are sandwiched between the expectations that your own mother had for you and the expectations you have for your own daughter. These dual expectations are framed by your past and resonate, creating a vulnerability and sensitivity to your daughter's judgments about you as well as your judgments about her. You may find yourself wanting to please your own mother and daughter at the same time.

So many mothers in our focus groups perceived that their mothers were hard to please. This experience naturally affects the expectations they have for their daughters. One mother said, "My daughter hates anything matching, anything too fashionable. When I bought an adorable sweater, she rolled her eyes in judgment and said, 'Do you think you should be wearing that?' I must admit, it took the joy out of the purchase and her remark made me self-conscious. I snapped back and said, 'My God, Christine, my own mother was never as critical as you.'" The most important homework we can do to help our daughters is, first, to recognize and manage our own baggage, which includes understanding our relationships with our own mothers. How many times do you hear yourself saying, "I never thought I'd say that; I sound just like my mother"?

Understanding how your mother responded to you during adolescence will affect how you respond to your daughter. Was your mother rigid or flexible? Was she supportive or restrictive? Could you count on her support, or did she rely on you for support? Was your mother happy, depressed, optimistic, or pessimistic? How do all or some of these affect your mothering? Leslie, the mother of Maggie, said, "My mother never gave me breathing room. She lived and died for the details of my life. Every morsel of gossip seemed to feed her, and I felt like I was suffocating.

"As Maggie reached adolescence, I remembered the feeling I had when my mother would ask me a million questions about the day and was never satisfied with 'Nothing happened, Mom.' So, while I'm dying to know the same things about Maggie's life, I consciously hold back. I think I'm giving her permission to have some sense of privacy in her life and know that not everything has to be shared. What's difficult for me is figuring whether by stepping back, I'm getting too far away from sharing Maggie's life." Leslie wrestles with understanding appropriate boundaries because she is trying to avoid replicating her mother's smothering and hovering.

It is a good idea to be somewhat reflective and to gain some understanding of your own childhood so that you can guide your daughter better. Otherwise, you may keep replaying old tapes, and what worked or didn't work for you won't necessarily work for your daughter. You have to adapt. What is going to work depends on reflecting on each individual's personal needs and experience. Get ready for the rolling eyes and back talk.

Know Your Own Relationship with Your Mother

When we evaluate our own relationship with our mothers, we can identify what was joyous, painful, destructive, and enriching. Cassie, a 43-year-old mother of two teenage girls, said, "My mother was very intellectually insecure. On the other hand, school was the place I thrived because academics came easy for me. The more I achieved, the more I felt I was betraying my mother. Instead of enjoying my success, my mother felt diminished by it and frequently made snide comments about me being too smart and too full of myself. It took many years for me to understand that I had the right to be proud of my accomplishments."

In this case, Cassie's mother let her own insecurity interfere with enjoying her daughter's achievement, and, as a result, Cassie couldn't enjoy her own success. When Cassie's daughter Alison struggled with school and was diagnosed with learning disabilities, Cassie both sympathized with her own mother's struggle with learning and mourned the fact that she never had the emotional support from her mother that she now gives to Alison.

Many of our parenting decisions are made in reaction to something uncomfortable that we experienced as a daughter. Kathleen, the mother of Stella, said, "When I was a new mother, of course I wasn't sleeping, and when I'm sleep-deprived it is all I can think about. When I complained about the exhaustion to my mother, she said very off-handedly, 'Kathleen, nobody ever died from lack of sleep.' Although I know her comments weren't mean-spirited, what I was looking for was a little empathy. All she had to say was, 'It's hard to be tired.' I wasn't really looking for anything else but an opportunity to express myself and be understood.

"My mother would constantly offer what I'm sure she felt was simply advice to improve my child rearing. For example, 'Kathleen, you really shouldn't be giving Stella a snack; it's too close to dinner,' or 'Put long pants on her when she rides her bicycle.' Although my mother felt that her advice was helpful, I heard it as judgmental and critical. Only over time did I develop more insight, and my relationship with my mother improved. I experienced her 'constructive criticism' as less hurtful."

Kathleen continued, "My experience with my mother has taught me many things. First, I learned to be careful not to misinterpret complaining and to be more respectful when my daughter expresses her discomforts. Second, to be aware that advice is not necessarily heard as positive and constructive." Kathleen learned to validate her daughter's feelings by paying attention to her own past and changing some behaviors that frustrated her as a daughter. Understanding the past provides you, as a mother, with knowledge and insights that will enable you to be less reactive and to think before you speak. The truth is that there is no objective reality. What is important is that you understand how you felt as a daughter and adjust your parenting to maximize the positive feelings you experienced and minimize the negative feelings.

Setting Boundaries

With self-awareness you can distinguish more readily between your own issues and those of your daughter. However, even with this clarity, your daughter's problems are still emotionally challenging. One challenge is determining how to set appropriate boundaries. If you don't take the time to understand where you leave off and your daughter begins, you are much more likely to behave inconsistently. Boundaries give your daughter a clear understanding of your limits, what you want, how you feel, and how you see the world.

There are two kinds of boundaries related to each girl's development of a sense of self. One is providing your daughter with the necessary space and privacy she needs to begin to become her own person (individuate). The second boundary involves giving your daughter permission to speak her mind and express uncomfortable feelings, including anger and aggression. Establishing these boundaries will contribute to the development of mutual respect between parents and daughters, as well as to your daughter's sense of self.

Without exception, as we see the issues that our daughters grapple with, we vacillate between the concern that comes from our own baggage and the fears that apply to our daughters. For example, if you tell your daughter she looks sad and your daughter answers, "Mom, nothing is wrong," most mothers have a hard time taking this at face value and believing that there really isn't a problem. Sometimes girls just don't want to share what's on their minds, and sometimes there really *is* nothing to share.

Madison, a ninth grader, said, "Mom, I'm going to tell you something about why I'm so upset with Josh, but I don't want to have to tell you everything." Her mother said, "After hearing only half the story, although I was left feeling that something was wrong, I accepted what Madison said. I went along with her request, selfishly, because I wanted to keep the communication channel open and also because I wanted to honor her privacy." Because the expectation is for daughters to spill their guts, mothers miss the opportunity to adhere to boundaries and give their daughters a chance to individuate. Often when girls do spill their guts, we have to puzzle through to find out what's really up.

This can be a painful process because so many mothers are overly invested in their daughters' lives. They feel their daughters' pain from social rejection and ask to be included in daily details that should be left unknown. Rita, the mother of a high school freshman, said, "This year was so much better than middle school," as if she had experienced the school year herself. Overinvolvement gives your daughter the unintended message that you don't have confidence in her ability to be self-sufficient and to solve problems for herself. This involvement also provides an unnecessary layer of emotions to confront for both you and your daughter.

Healthy boundaries help you to step back and separate your own experience from that of your daughter. Certainly, there are times when you impose standards that are fair and appropriate, even though your daughter may disagree. However, it is important for you to keep from imposing your own agenda when it doesn't respect your daughter's thoughts and feelings about what is good for her versus what may be more appropriate for you. This distance—this engaged detachment—provides girls with the space to grow into their own women, not "Shrinky Dinks" of their moms. By setting appropriate boundaries with your daughter, you are modeling what she can expect for herself in all other relationships. In today's child-focused world, it is too easy to lose perspective.

Mothers need to differentiate themselves from their daughters. This separation is critical to provide your daughter with space to grow and develop during adolescence. It is natural for girls to remain connected to their mothers, which makes this process of separation more difficult. If the relationship does not allow room for daughters to become independent, they will not be able to develop a strong sense of self. Eventually they *will* need to separate from their mothers, otherwise there may be potential damage to the mother-daughter relationship.

To have healthy relationships, daughters need help from their mothers to understand that differentiating from one's mother is normal and good. It's helpful to remember that mothers have the opportunity to validate their teenage daughters' changing self. According to Judy Mann, author of *The Difference: Growing Up Female in America*, "When girls don't spend their twenties in recovery from an adolescence that drives them into a search for autonomy from mothers—a search that almost inevitably catapults them into dependency on men," they end up with a more satisfying relationship based on reciprocal caring and respect.

Daughters as Rivals

When girls are in their prime, their mothers' youth is diminishing, and many women are struggling to retain their self-esteem. Mothers often fail to recognize and discuss feelings of competition with their daughters. Janine said, "Dealing with my own middle age, while my daughter is blossoming and youthful, is tough, especially when the shorts that they are showing now are no bigger than a parenthesis. They barely cover my butt. I want to express myself through fashion, but I struggle with balancing my desire to look cool with appropriateness. I don't want to look frumpy. Where is the middle ground?"

Margie, the mother of Lisa and Emily, said, "I no longer feel like eyes are on me when I enter a room; I have become invisible. Last month my family vacationed in Wyoming. When I was on a horse, nobody talked to me or noticed me. The horse wranglers talked to my husband, Peter, about riding technique and flirted with the girls. I felt like I was unseen. Thankfully, I talked with my girlfriends, and they really understood. We discussed how we no longer have to get outraged at men whistling and jeering at us on the street, because it doesn't happen anymore. My friends knew too well exactly what I was feeling." Talking with close friends helps us to face the effects of aging on self-esteem.

Discussion with friends helps you to learn that, among other things, accepting and acknowledging your own aging gracefully, rather than trying to look like and/or act like one of your daughter's friends, is healthy parenting. Barbara, the 49-year-old mother of two teenage girls, said, "My daughters dress like hippies. They wear peasant blouses and bell-bottoms. I feel kind of jaded when I tell them that I've been there and done that. The fact that it is not fresh and new for me forces me to confront my age and represents something that is gone, along with my youth. Somewhat cynically I've told them, 'Girls, each fashion craze should be experienced once in your lifetime. If it comes around again, like bell-bottoms or hot pants, you're too old to wear it.'" Humor is a good communication tool to avoid the competitiveness of "been there, done that."

It is damaging when you communicate your own unhappiness with and insecurity about your body to your daughter. Eighteen-year-old Rebecca said, "My mother is always talking about losing weight. She hates her thighs and talks about getting liposuction. Her arms look normal to me, but she would never let the light of day shine on her upper arms. I feel bad because I'm struggling myself. How can I learn to accept myself, warts and all, when my own mother can't relax about her body?" According to Joan Brumberg's *The Body Project*, many young women ask the same question. It is particularly difficult to nurture self-confident girls for mothers who are coping with negative feelings about their own bodies.

Daughters can be hypercritical of mothers. You need to understand that your daughter sees you through a child's lens. Becoming self-aware helps you to avoid being damaged or embarrassed by your daughter's scrutiny during the teenage years. For many moms, this scrutiny can begin much earlier than adolescence. Judith, the mother of four-year-old Hannah, said, "It's already started, and Hannah just turned four! Last night during dinner at a Chinese restaurant, Hannah turned to my sister and said, 'Aunt Sharon, did you see my mommy's pimple? Mom, show Aunt Sharon your pimple.'" For Judith, this triggered memories of her own mother constantly scrutinizing her face and suggesting that she use Clearasil, even when this lotion left a rash the shape of South America on her cheeks. It's easy to forget that your young daughter is only a child and is not really passing judgment. She is beginning to notice that she is separate from you. Try hard not to feel diminished in the face of the x-ray vision of your daughter. This kind of scrutiny continues through an extended period of adolescence.

Mothers need as much insight about themselves as possible. Because the messages girls get from our culture are so powerful and pervasive, threats to a girl's ability to be satisfied with herself are found everywhere. These threats are much more painful and damaging when a girl receives them from her mother as well. You can help your daughter resist and manage these cultural influences better if you show that you are comfortable with yourself. It's hard for a girl to absorb the idea that she is beautiful inside and out from you if you are openly dissatisfied with yourself. So be careful about how you express your own body image problems and related anxieties. If you have trouble doing that, try talking to friends instead, out of your daughter's hearing. If you continue to have difficulty and find yourself thinking negatively about your body and your looks regularly, it might be a good idea to seek counseling to avoid passing on your insecurities to your daughter.

Fathers and Daughters: Make Room for Daddy

Parenting roles and responsibilities are shared more now than at any other time in history. Just as girls' relationships with their mothers today are different from our experiences with our mothers, we see the same trend of increased involvement of fathers with their daughters. Dads want to be active in their daughters' lives and don't presume that they can't share activities and interests because they don't share the same gender. The interest that fathers have in their daughters' lives has an important impact. A father's relationship with his daughter creates the foundation for her ability to achieve her goals and serves as a model for relationships with other men. One daughter shares the mantra that her father repeated to her, "My dad always told me: 'If you dream it, you can do it.'"

Fathers are no longer satisfied with just being detached financial providers. Judy Mann reports that fathers play a "critical role in how high their daughters aspire and in girls' future relationships with boys and men. Fathers can enable their daughters to soar or they can cripple them into dependence." They are much more involved in the everyday details of their children's lives than were fathers of previous generations. We no longer hear dads saying, "I won't change a dirty diaper"; many men's rooms include baby-changing tables, and lots of dads know how to put barrettes and a ponytail holder in their daughters' hair. Many drive carpools, coach sports teams, and get involved in school by chaperoning field trips. One dad said, "I carpool to my daughter's ballet class, and it connects me to the details of her life. I hear stories and gossip in the car that help me understand the dynamics of her social scene." Mothers should help fathers stay connected to their daughters by supporting opportunities for them to be close. Encourage them to sometimes go and do things on their own.

Girls who have good relationships with their dads tend to consider themselves to be worthy of love. As a supportive and involved father, you model the relationship that a daughter can expect with her significant other. When you have expressed healthy affection, girls are more likely to expect a positive relationship. This confidence serves them well throughout their adult lives.

Dads and Achievement

Looking back on their childhoods, women who have achieved in nontraditional careers point to the expectations and encouragement of their fathers as key to their success. According to Joe Kelly in *The MentorGirl Voice* newsletter, the relationship between fathers and daughters and mothers and sons has a greater impact on self-esteem than the relationship with the same-sex parent. Brenda, who has one daughter, remembered the power of her father's unwavering belief: "In college I was accepted into the school of engineering. I enrolled and began what I thought was an extraordinary journey. Looking at the students in my first survey course, I counted three hundred five guys and four girls—me included. Only two of us got our degrees in engineering, and two dropped out. Sometimes I look back and wonder how I got through it. But in my heart, I know that I did it because my father believed I could. He never saw failure in anything I tried, and he continuously encouraged me to try anything and everything. It was my dad who recognized my math and science ability and ignored my college counselor's advice that I major in liberal arts. My dad helped me believe I could do it when less than 2 percent of my class were girls."

Carol, a 48-year-old mother of one daughter and two sons, reminisced, "I was an only child, and my father took me along to political demonstrations, chess club meetings, and to his office. The only time I was permitted to stay up late was to watch television with my dad, usually something like 'Hallmark Hall of Fame' or 'Playhouse 90' because he thought these shows were intellectual. My dad always assumed that I would finish college and suggested that I think about becoming a professional.

"At about 12 years old, I learned that many people had a different idea about the importance of education for a girl. When I was asked what I wanted to be when I grew up, my answers—a doctor, a scientist—always generated a chuckle or two. With a condescending tone, they always asked, 'What type of man would you like to marry when you grow up?' I remember a great feeling of indignation coming over me. How dare they ignore my dreams and pigeonhole me? My dad never did that. He stood in stark contrast to the discouraging messages that I received from other people. When the world around me said, 'Carol, don't get ahead of yourself; keep your dreams simple,' my dad showed me the way to stay in touch with greater possibilities." As a father, you should take great satisfaction in the importance of your support for your daughter's ambitions and dreams.

A significant strategy to help your daughter achieve is for you to learn what your daughter is interested in and use this knowledge to encourage and motivate her. In her article titled, "Single-Minded, Even a Daughter Can Want to Be Just Like Dad," Jane Ganahl writes about her dad, "[My dad] took each daughter's talents and strengthened them. So I, as a tomboyish little girl, must have perplexed him a bit. I mean, what do fathers do who have two girls who are the epitome of femininity and one who is quite the opposite? Do what my dad did, I guess, and figure out a way to nurture the talents with which the offspring sprung. While my sisters were putting on puppet shows or cooking, I'd be outside with my brother Rob, roaming the hills of Woodside, . . . scraping my knobby knees climbing trees. My dad showed me how to nail pieces of wood into the tree so I could climb up more handily."

Sexuality: A Difficult Subject for Dads

While there are many opportunities for fathers to enjoy their girls, the teen years are especially trying for dads because of their daughters' sexual development. Our culture sexualizes young girls at increasingly earlier ages, long before dads are ready to accept these changes, which tends to make both dads and daughters self-conscious. Fathers miss the physical closeness that they experienced when their daughters were young and may feel inhibited about being as physically demonstrative with their developing adolescents.

More than mothers, dads are uncomfortable about seeing their daughters as sexual beings. Dads have a hard time with their daughters' growing up. In the focus groups we conducted, every father had a story about his shock and disapproval when his young teenage daughter began dressing for a Saturday night in an outfit that he felt belonged on someone years older. One father said, "Seeing my little girl dressed in a ridiculously short skirt and skimpy top made me so uncomfortable that I felt like forbidding her from going out of the house until she was 21! Of course my wife thought I was overreacting, but who knew the mind of an adolescent boy better than me?"

Your daughter looks to you for approval of her accomplishments *and* her looks. You need to respect your daughter's development into a young woman and reflect a positive view of how she looks. Michael, the father of 16-year-old Jessica, said, "I tell and show my Jessica that I love her for who she is as a whole person, not just as either a pretty or smart girl, but as a young woman who is capable of being both attractive and bright. I make sure to let her know that I think she's beautiful inside and out." As your daughter becomes a sexual being, you must work to figure out a way to at least *appear* to be comfortable with this transition. Ready or not, little girls develop into young women whom young men find attractive.

During these years, it's important for you to understand the tremendous impact you can have, positive and negative, on your daughter's self-image. This stage of development is a bad time to tease her about her body. Loren, a college junior, told us that she remembers standing in front of the kitchen refrigerator and looking for something to eat when her father teased her by puffing out his cheeks in Dizzy Gillespie fashion. She noted that although it was a small moment, it was *the* moment that she decided to hide. Loren remembers this gesture and how it made her feel shame about her eating. Loren's example demonstrates how nonverbal, as well as verbal, comments carry enough power to affect how your daughter feels about her body.

You have a unique opportunity to contribute to your daughter's appreciation of her body, and she is more likely to be physically active if she participates in sports with you. Play catch with her, take walks, jog, encourage team sports, do anything and everything that will help her to understand how to use her body in a positive and healthy way. According to "Ten Tips for Dads of Daughters" on the website Dads and Daughters, girls who are physically active are "less likely to get pregnant, drop out of school, or put up with abuse. The most physically active girls have fathers who are active with them!" Be careful about commenting about your daughter's weight, be positive about her appearance without making it seem overly important, and praise her accomplishments. Your approval will help her to build high self-esteem.

Daddy's Girl

We do want to mention one caveat regarding father-daughter relationships. It is natural for fathers to want to protect their daughters; however, too much protection can create a pattern of dependency. When girls are treated like "daddy's princess" or "little girl," they are more likely to continue dependent behavior. Fathers can slide into this role very easily because, unlike with boys, our culture encourages protection of girls. Girls need to feel that they can rely on their dads; they also need to feel that they can take care of and assert themselves in the world. Mothers and fathers both need to be mindful of the negative effects of too much coddling.

Fathers face their own challenges in raising their daughters. We believe Judy Mann provided an exceptionally clear approach to these issues in her book *The Difference* when she said, "Give her something other than love. Give her admiration and respect for how she thinks and how she handles herself." This message helps to build resilient girls, girls with character and strength.

Divorce and Single Parents: Separate and Equal

Divorce is never easy, regardless of your daughter's age. All parents struggle with how to minimize the impact of new family configurations on their children. While many of you worry that your child will feel as if he or she is the only one, today's reality is that an extraordinarily large number of children are raised by single parents or parents living apart with joint custody.

While we don't want to sanitize the pain associated with divorce, we want to stress that children can thrive in divorced families that promote healthy and honest communication. Jill, a 17-year-old high school junior, remembered, "I always felt more comfortable at my mom's house. It was easier for me to talk to her because she was more flexible than my dad and we shared so many common interests. In the fall, when my mother first got depressed, she and my dad said it was best for me to spend more time at my dad's house.

"At first this was hard for me because I was very reluctant to share much with my dad. I found him stuffy and silent and never knew what he was thinking. But my mother really encouraged me to trust that he was interested in my life and made me promise that I'd keep trying to connect, because he sure was trying. The next half year was transformative for me. I developed a relationship with my father that I would never have had. While I always knew that my dad loved me, I never felt known by my dad. I now have a close relationship with both my mom and my dad."

Jill's story demonstrates how, sometimes, children as well as parents find themselves in uncomfortable patterns that become difficult to break. Even though her dad was trying to get close to her, Jill found it hard to warm to his attempts. Jill's mother's illness, combined with her mother's desire to encourage her daughter to communicate with her dad and her dad's perseverance, created a win-win situation for everyone.

Even though you may try to make the transition as easy as possible, many girls feel that they don't have a comfortable home base. Girls also may feel they are displaced whenever they visit their noncustodial parent. Mia, a 15-year-old, said, "My mother is straight out of Talbots: we have ruffles on pillows and some pillows have pillows. I don't think I've ever sat on the living room couch. My room looks like it's out of a magazine when all I want is a mattress on the floor. Needless to say, I'm not really free to be myself at Mom's. But at my dad's, it's a 180-degree difference. My room really looks like me. I've got posters taped on the walls, and he never says I'm ruining the paint. I light incense and candles. It's really cool."

The differences in Mia's two worlds create conflict for her regarding her feelings for her parents. Mia's parents have such different styles that she tends to discount her mother's rather than communicating her discomfort. Like many kids, Mia doesn't want to exacerbate an already difficult situation. With a divorced family, communication is more loaded than it would be otherwise, but it certainly can be done successfully.

Married parents don't always agree on how to parent, and divorce complicates parenting further. Divorced parents have to prioritize

"Constance Ahrons reports, 'There is an accumulating body of knowledge based on many studies that show only minor differences between children of divorce and those from intact families, and the great majority of children with divorced parents reach adulthood to lead reasonably fulfilling lives.'"
—KAREN S. PETERSON, "Kids of Divorced Parents Straddle a Divided World"

issues and negotiate compromises independent of their separation. In divorce, individuals can no longer take communication and cooperation for granted. Everyone has to make a real effort to communicate what is truly important. Although living in two separate homes, parents must try to maintain consistent messages in child raising.

To be successful, you must negotiate agreements based on a set of core values and stick by them. This is not easy to accomplish, but it is vital to make children feel comfortable with both parents. The way you behave as a couple and handle conflict models how relationships work in a family. By compromising and demonstrating willingness to give and take, you and your spouse become positive role models for your daughter. Except in extreme situations, such as abuse and neglect, parents have a responsibility to support and encourage their daughter's relationship with the other parent.

There is some good news for divorced mothers of girls. Depending on how well their mothers handle divorce, most girls survive and grow up to become confident and competent adults, according to Mavis Hetherington's "Virginia Longitudinal Study of Divorce," in *For Better or for Worse: Divorce Reconsidered.* Among her findings was that, despite economic hardship, many women reported doing better after the divorce. They attributed this to having to cope with difficulty and being forced to develop new competencies in the aftermath of the divorce. In fact, two years after divorce, Hetherington found that women are less depressed than those who remain in combative, unhappy marriages. Girls can benefit from observing this transformation in their mothers.

While many factors contribute to creating a nurturing environment, one factor more than others contributes to creating a toxic environment. Conflict has a negative effect on children, regardless of their parents' marital status. Therefore, your goal should be to keep conflict at a minimum and to make a conscious effort to keep your child out of the fray. According to the Association of Family and Conciliation Courts, as a child of divorced parents, your daughter has rights that include these:

* The right to maintain a relationship with both mom and dad without witnessing either parent's hurt or anger
* The right to be free from battles, free of becoming a messenger between parents or being asked to spy on the other parent
* The right to all of the extended relationships, grandparents, cousins, and family friends who were important to her before the divorce
* The right to be a child without having to behave like a miniparent and assume parental roles
* The right to maintain extracurricular activities and relationships with friends without having to fear losing time with one parent

Single-Parent Homes

Rather than arguing that the only healthy family is a two-parent family, you need to look at what your child needs to develop to his or her maximum potential. What all children need is one communicative and emotionally intelligent parent—an engaged parent who cultivates a positive, strong relationship.

We believe that successful single-parent households have much to teach us and that children can flourish in a single-parent home. In general, children have only one set of rules in families headed by a single-parent mother or father, so the rules stay the rules without lengthy bickering between parents. Rules, such as "no TV after 10:00 P.M.," remain consistent.

In single-parent homes, children are presented with opportunities to contribute to the family because they have more occasions to pitch in and help. Their increased involvement in chores creates an environment that promotes responsibility and competence. Children thrive with the knowledge that they have something to offer in addition to staying out of trouble and getting good grades. Getting children to do chores is challenging, but chores provide opportunities for family participation and for building children's self-esteem.

Single-parent households call for one parent to provide both the nurturing and managerial functions. This merging of skills can be beneficial for girls because they see their mothers functioning as the head of a household, performing all the roles required to run the home. Similarly, girls benefit from seeing their dads in the role of nurturer as well as provider. Those of you who model more flexible roles offer your daughters a broader range of competencies.

Moms and Dads: Listening Through the Noise

One thing we all agree on is that relationships with teenage daughters are often trying and difficult. Even when we exercise tremendous effort, we often receive little positive feedback. A happy time can disintegrate into a door-slamming episode in a heartbeat. Often, it's easier to throw up your hands and give in in the face of arguments that feel like filibusters. Take heart in knowing that drama, insults, and criticism are all part of your daughter's drive to become independent. A normal part of developing autonomy is testing limits and boundaries. Even though it sometimes feels that your daughter doesn't want you around, she still needs your guidance. Continue to make yourself available, remain supportive, and persist in sharing your values and expectations.

To support your daughter, try a skill we call "engaged detachment," which requires close involvement but with a sense of perspective. Engaged parenting includes being empathetic, acting as a sounding board, and providing objective coaching. Detached parenting requires parents to step back from the immediate moment and remember the big picture. The following example illustrates this concept.

Your daughter comes home from a soccer game and is disappointed and unhappy about the amount of playing time she is getting. Your job would be to listen to her complaints, be empathetic about how hard it must be for her, and help her to strategize ways of handling the disappointment. You may even want to give her suggestions about how she may improve her skills and make that effort known to the coach. You are not as concerned about the amount of playing time she receives as about how she uses the experience to grow and mature. The benefits of this experience would include your daughter learning how to advocate for herself in appropriate ways, being realistic about her expectations, and taking responsibility for her participation on the team. You may want to confront the coach, but your more important job is teaching and giving your daughter opportunities to learn and practice life skills while not being attached to the outcome.

It's vital to stay connected to your daughter while giving her the space to be mindful of what she is doing. This approach also allows your daughter to mature while learning to make her own assessments free from a disabling dependence. This practice provides her with what Bert Adams calls, in "Change and Continuity in the U.S. Family Today," "sponsored independence," which helps her to develop her own inner compass and ultimately leads to self-reliance.

As part of a generation that has worked so hard to effect immense change in gender roles, work, and sexuality, your complex involvement in your child's adolescence is not surprising. We've worked hard to give our daughters more options and choices, and we want them to take advantage of every possible opportunity. This hyperinvolvement in the details of our children's lives gives us a different perspective from our parents'. It's not that we love our children any more than our parents loved us; it's just that our parents were less involved and often had more limited expectations, especially for girls. One mother told the story of her parents taking her to her first day of kindergarten and not returning to her school until high school graduation. She said, "In my childhood, the only parents who went to school went to pick up their kids from after-school detention." By contrast, contemporary parents have a deep reservoir of curiosity about and interest in child raising.

As moms and dads, you have a responsibility to talk with your daughters about what it means to come of age in a society where authentic self-expression for girls and women is far more complicated than choosing whether you like Britney Spears or Christina Aguilera. As much as adolescents mirror the obsessions of contemporary culture, you remain by far the most significant influence in your child's development. You have a unique set of experiences and skills that enables you to counsel and guide your teenage daughter. At times it may seem as if adolescence will never end, but adolescence is just another stage in the process of parenting. Someday your daughter's body will stop changing, her brain will calm down, and you will be rewarded with a balanced relationship with a young woman who loves you.

8

Passing on Our Stories

Helping Our Daughters to Appreciate the Women
Who Made Today's Opportunities Happen

"Because we must tell and retell, learn and relearn, these women's stories, and we must make it our personal mission, in our everyday lives, to pass these stories on to our daughters and sons. Because we cannot—and must not—ever forget that the rights and responsibilities we enjoy as women today were not just bestowed upon us by some benevolent ruler. They were fought for, agonized over, marched for, jailed for, and even died for by brave and persistent women and men who came before us."

—HILLARY RODHAM CLINTON
on the 150th anniversary of the first
women's rights convention, 1998

The past 35 years have seen enormous changes in the way women view themselves in our society. According to Cynthia Harrison's 2003 article "From the Home to the House: The Changing Role of Women in American Society":

> The right of a woman to work outside the home is no longer in question, especially since most families with two parents depend on a second income. Some 60 percent of wives now work for wages. With her own income, the American woman today is in the position to exercise more authority within her home or to end an unhappy marriage. Although the movement into formal political office has been gradual since women won the vote in 1920, women have become more visible and central political actors. Women's issues—sex discrimination, reproductive rights, care of children, economic equity across sex and racial lines—get full attention from policy makers. Federal law has established a woman's right to equal treatment in schools and in the workplace and women have taken advantage of these opportunities.

With all of these advances and this personal freedom brought about by the women's movement, girls still face complex problems. In contrast to the past, when there were more commonly accepted expectations for girls, today they often lack clear-cut rules, role models, or guidelines when considering the range of choices available to them.

Along with air travel and the microchip, some would say that the women's movement was a defining event of the 20th century. However, to a large degree, many benefits have been won as recently as the past two decades. The changes are still so fresh that adult women and their teenage daughters are adapting simultaneously to the resulting transformation in social roles and increased opportunities. Their simultaneous labors have had unintended consequences. Flush with newly won victories, adult women must confront the challenges of autonomy in midlife, while at the same time raising teenagers.

Our focus groups revealed that many mothers are still struggling to manage their own independence while simultaneously trying to be useful role models and provide guidance for their daughters. Mothers who are engaged in this transition may be emotionally less available for their children at a time when their daughters need direction in their own efforts to negotiate their autonomy and independence. A daughter who needs direction may find her mother's preoccupation with her own issues to be a source of loss, disappointment, and resentment. Admiration for their mothers' accomplishments often comes later, when daughters begin to see their mothers as human beings separate from themselves. For daughters whose mothers overidentify with them, their mothers' independence may be a welcome relief.

However, our daughters still require and compete for our attention. It's imperative that we remain engaged as parents while we seek our own way. Communication and connection are vital. We must acknowledge our mutual challenges and understand that mothers and daughters experience the same issues but from different vantage points. However, most important of all, we must always be present for our daughters, despite the demands of our own issues. We must help our daughters to see the struggle for independence from both historical and contemporary perspectives.

We believe that a young girl's life warrants examination within historical context. Over the past 35 years, the daily activities of girls' lives have changed. This has affected the perceptions of social roles and life expectations for girls. In the process of growing up, our daugh-

"Like the inevitable merging of river into sea, sea into ocean, our lives are connected with those of our ancestors. Through these bonds, we discover what contributes to the way we are today, what ties we have to the past, and how to strengthen ourselves for the future."

—ASIAN WOMEN UNITED OF CALIFORNIA, *Making Waves: An Anthology of Writings by and About Asian American Women*

ters have many more choices than we did at their age. They have more opportunities but at the same time still address difficult questions. Understanding the historical significance of the recent changes in the role of women in our society gives perspective that assists our ability to effectively mentor our daughters.

"I Wanna Be Bobby's Girl"

"I Wanna Be Bobby's Girl," the singer in the 1950s song pleaded, "that's the most important thing to me." If one were to believe the magazines, songs, and many of the books that appeared during this decade, being someone's "girl" was indeed the most important goal an American female could seek. Today, daily life is different for many women. However, many girls think that the way they live now is the way it always was. If we don't share our history, our daughters will be unaware of what a sea change has occurred in the past 30 or 40 years for women.

Many mothers remember what it was like for them when they were younger. Debbie, the mother of a 19-year-old daughter, remembered being sent home from ninth grade because her skirt was too short: "I don't remember who reported me, but I was sent to the principal's office, where someone manually pressed the skirt against my kneecap and found that it was in violation of the school's 'your skirt must cover your knee' code. I had to walk almost a mile home to change. When I tell my daughter about the myriad rules for girls she rolls her eyes in disbelief."

Another mother said, "We were expected to put on a skirt or dress for dinner in my dorm freshman year. How ridiculous. Most girls were wearing jeans, so they'd have to go to their rooms and change for meals. One clever student started a business making these awful corduroy sacks that we called 'meal jumpers.' It was OK to wear a corduroy potato sack but not pants. We also had curfews with pretty serious consequences, and the boys didn't. Everywhere there were different standards for girls than there were for boys. In the effort to 'protect' our virginity, we had to abide by different standards than boys did. Even after leaving home, we were considered to be in need of protection and not left on our own."

Mothers in our focus groups talked about how the changes we see today were not won easily. Even changing something as simple as restrictive dress codes was a struggle. One mother remembered, "During my first year of teaching in 1972, women teachers had to wear skirts or dresses. This was particularly hard for teachers of elementary students who needed to spend much of their time sitting on the floor. I remember being as concerned about whether my crotch was showing as whether the ducklings in *Make Way for Ducklings* made it safely across the road. I worked with the teacher's union and had to go to the school board to change the dress code. Only then could we get incremental changes. For the first year we wore polyester pantsuits because they looked more like a man's suit. There was no model for professional women that included pants." These are important stories to share with our daughters. If they don't know their history, they'll take it for granted and may lose hard-won rights.

Perspective: The Women's Rights Movement

The women's movement of the mid-1960s through 1980s challenged and sometimes changed virtually every aspect of U.S. society, including education, law and policy, the workplace, the political process, familial relations, religious practices, and the production of culture—literature, art, television, music, and the movies. Betty Friedan's *The Feminine Mystique* provided a powerful analysis of discontent among white, well-educated housewives with no appropriate outlets for their talents and energies. Friedan observed that during the 1950s there were almost no articles or stories about women involved outside

"Yes, I think sometimes with unlimited opportunity comes unlimited pressure, not that I would give up the opportunity."
—Focus group mom

their homes. Almost all fiction conveyed the same message to readers: a man and a family were the only legitimate interests healthy women should have.

As Hillary Rodham Clinton remarked at the 150th anniversary of the first women's rights convention, the only way our daughters will understand and appreciate the advances they have inherited is to "tell and retell . . . women's stories," women's history. While most history textbooks simply state that "women were given the right to vote in 1920," women's stories provide a different perspective. Winning the vote for women took decades of lobbying Congress, years of organizing state referendum campaigns, months of picketing in front of the White House, millions of dollars raised, thousands of women actively involved, dozens of parades, and numerous arrests. Women were not given the right to vote; they were forced to wage one of the longest and toughest voting rights campaigns in history.

Does your daughter also know that just 35 years ago married women were not issued credit cards in their own name? Most women could not get a bank loan without a male cosigner. Does she know that women automatically lost their name and had to legally change their name back to their maiden name if they wished to use it the day after they were married? When the Equal Pay Act was passed in 1963, women earned only 58 cents for every dollar men earned. Alicia Lange reports in "The Family Gap: Do Mothers Earn Less?" that this pay gap is disappearing at a rate of approximately 10 cents every 20 to 30 years. Generations of women have worked to give our daughters the opportunities they now enjoy. Unfortunately, many girls, as well as some of their mothers, still know very little about the history of the female experience; they are only spectators.

With knowledge, girls have the opportunity to see themselves and their connection to this historic process differently. Because they view the past in a new light, they are able to see new possibilities in the present and an enriched vision for what is to come. They gain an appreciation for what came before them, and they take more responsibility in shaping their own future. Their mothers also take pride in their accomplishments.

Helene told the following story: "It has been my pleasure to watch my teenage daughter swim competitively, water ski, bowl, play basketball and baseball, ride bikes, run, and bench press. And it has been my quiet revenge that five-foot-two-inch Holly, petite and pretty, has done these things without ever damaging her 'fragile internal organs' or losing her femininity."

Even in spite of these changes, challenges still exist. One of the major issues your daughter faces is how to balance the conflicts that arise from the increased opportunities available to her. She must learn to match her need to connect and have family and other intimate relationships with her life outside of the family. This life may include career, volunteer work, and other independent activities. The challenge is in how she will incorporate these new expectations with the more traditional roles for which women have always been responsible.

Women are not being asked to give up their old social roles; they are expected to add new roles to an already full plate. Increased expectations create conflicts for daughters as well as their mothers. We still don't have all the answers, and not all women have choices. There are and have always been women who must balance motherhood and career, because their families depend on their income.

These new expectations require your daughter to form new patterns in her relationships with her significant others. They also allow her the freedom to be more financially independent, which accounts for young women marrying at a later age or choosing not to stay with a spouse for financial reasons alone. With opportunity comes responsibility and compromise. Just as we talk to our girls about different college majors and career choices, we must discuss the realities of how to balance a personal and professional life. This is where our experience can make a difference.

Today's Challenges

Modern society has created more educational and career opportunities for women. Along with these advances, however, we are still saddled with an unrealistic and unattainable ideal of the perfect female. Unfortunately, the emphasis is on looks rather than character. The extent to which teenage girls and women have starved themselves physically and obsessed psychologically in recent decades has robbed them of the opportunity to develop parts of themselves that reject this impossible ideal.

Naomi Wolf writes that women need to understand they are robbing themselves of their full potential in order to feed a multibillion-dollar industry that fuels the insecurities of women and girls. She states, "A century ago, Nora slammed the door of the doll's house; a generation ago, women turned their backs on the consumer heaven of the isolated, multiapplianced home; but where women are trapped today, there is no door to slam." One mom said that she remembers events, weddings, and trips by how well she felt she fit into her clothes and looked in the photos. This preoccupation takes up too much space in the lives of women and girls. This beauty ideal is so insidious, it is ironic that even those who write and lecture about this topic struggle constantly to break free of it.

In spite of all the changes, reports Nancy Snyderman in *Girl in the Mirror*, "Girls still wrestle with the dichotomy between the old messages of femininity and the new messages of be all you want to be." As a result, girls can be confused and overwhelmed by having so

"I learned a history not then written in books but one passed from generation to generation on the steps of moonlit porches and beside dying fires in one-room houses."

—MILDRED D. TAYLOR, *Roll of Thunder, Hear My Cry*

many choices. You can help your daughter by encouraging her to consider career options based on goals she has set for her future life. This may mean that she wants to consider careers in the context of whether or not she decides to get married or have children. If women choose to have a career and a family, they, like men, should be able to have both.

One young woman in medical school told us that she chose her specialty because it provided her with more flexibility and balance in her personal life. Each career choice has different expectations that require compromise. Many young lawyers are faced with the choice of "mommy track" or "partner track," which makes it hard to strike a balance. Your daughter will benefit from conversations that give her permission to consider balance at the beginning of her decision making.

Society will benefit when both men and women have opportunities that enable them to have a satisfying career as well as a fulfilling family life, without having to sacrifice one for the other. This goal will help to lessen the pressure on girls, which has increased, because the expectations of being a super woman have trickled down to the next generation of girls.

Women have made substantial progress. Yet, the landscape for young women remains complicated. In her book *The Difference: Growing Up Female in America*, Judy Mann tells about her daughter, Katherine, who at 12 saw that her world was filled with inequalities for women. She sought Carol Gilligan's advice about what to tell Katherine. Gilligan advised, "Tell her that she's right, things are not all that

great for women, but that together, you and she will make a difference." There is great potential for improvement, but any view of the
future for teenage girls must be optimistic and credible and not ideal-
istic. Their future must also reflect the lessons of our history.

FAMILY MESSAGES

We all carry family messages with us that help to form our values. Think about
what messages or information you received when you were growing up from
your mother and other adult women and from your father and other adult
men about the following issues:

Family connection
Friendship
Success in school
Appearance
Using drugs or alcohol
Having sex
Marriage
Career
Children
Community responsibility
Acceptance of differences

After thinking about these issues, determine what messages you will or
do send your children about them. This will provide insight into not only what
you say but how you communicate messages to your daughter and will
strengthen your connection.

9

13 Strategic Solutions for Parents of Adolescent Girls

"The giving of love is an education in itself."

—ELEANOR ROOSEVELT

Next to being a teenager, parenting teenagers is one of the most unsettling of life's experiences. Adolescence is a time when girls are learning how to make independent decisions and judgments in an environment that calls for ever greater maturity. During this critical time, the guidance and support you provide help to determine how well your daughter navigates and responds to the myriad challenges she faces. As we have said before—but bears repeating—even though your daughter may not appear to want your involvement, adolescent girls really do want their parents' approval and support. You have to hang in there with your daughter and provide her with the love she needs to become a resilient adult.

In our focus groups, we met too many lovely and accomplished girls who frequently felt diminished by society's expectations. For example, body image and dissatisfaction with appearance came up in so many discussions with moms and daughters that we feel compelled to mention this issue in almost every chapter of the book. To tackle this critical issue, you must address your own demons first. You should try to refrain from asking your daughter questions that reinforce negative stereotypes, such as, "Do I look fat?" Mothers who have a hard time accepting themselves can't present a credible message about self-acceptance. As Marshall McLuhan said so many years ago, "The medium is the message."

What we heard from teenage girls is that you have to be careful about how you deliver messages; otherwise they can elicit the opposite effect. Messages about being overweight can cause girls to eat more rather than less. The same is true for underweight girls. Ultimately, healthy girls have to make changes for their own reasons, not because their mom or dad (or media messages) want them to. And above all, remember that, whatever your intent, children learn by example.

Although strategies are interspersed throughout this book, we have summarized them here for easy reference. Try not to be overwhelmed by the number of strategies; no one expects you to use them perfectly or all at one time! We have formulated these strategies from our focus groups, from conclusions we have drawn from our experience as mothers, and from working with girls in a professional capacity. We believe that you can use these strategies to smooth—although never eliminate—the inevitable bumps in the road.

1. Help your daughter to develop her own personal compass and build her authentic self.

✳ Stress the importance of integrity and establishing a moral center. Having a moral center provides your daughter with her own personal compass, which will enable her to judge her own behavior. Having integrity requires that she be accountable for her decisions. Only by being accountable can she develop self-respect.

* Provide opportunities for your daughter to build her self-esteem. For example, give her responsibilities as a family member to shovel snow, mow the lawn, take out the garbage, take care of younger siblings, and/or wash the dishes. Praise her when she does a good job, and emphasize the things she does well. If she makes a mistake, provide her with ideas for how to improve, rather than simply criticizing her. Genuine support and respect will help your daughter to gain self-confidence.

* Provide opportunities for your daughter to find her passion and identify her strengths, talents, and interests. Highlight what is special about her. Every girl has talents and unique qualities, and your recognition of these traits contributes to your daughter's self-worth.

* Promote independence and encourage independent thinking. Reward your daughter for speaking her mind. Give her opportunities to stretch that will give her confidence to think for herself. Girls who are always trying to be popular are less likely to give themselves permission to make a personal assessment.

* Give your daughter the skills to respond to tough situations. For example, ask her the following questions when considering solutions to her problems:

— What are the facts?
— What are my personal values?
— Does this fit with who I want to be?
— What questions should I ask?
— Where or to whom can I go for help?

* Support your daughter's presenting herself in an authentic way rather than in opposition to others just for the sake of opposition because she doesn't fit in. Assess whether your daughter is acting differently because she *is* different or if she is protecting herself from feeling like an outsider.

2. Listen to your daughter and see life through her eyes.

✳ Be mindful of the distinction between what girls say and what they really mean.

✳ Avoid preaching; slow down and listen rather than talk. For example, you may be worried about her social life, but she may be happy with just a few friends and not going out very much. However, if your daughter says she has no friends and she is miserable, then you may want to take a more proactive approach and get her some social-skills coaching. Skills coaching can be found in community organizations such as Big Sisters, Girl Scouts, and religious institutions and through school counselors and other mental health professionals.

✳ Help your daughter to keep her voice by listening to and validating her feelings. Validating her feelings tells her that she makes sense; it doesn't mean you agree with them.

✳ Share common experiences with your daughter (e.g., normalizing frustration, such as the late or early onset of puberty), but avoid reliving your own experiences through your daughter. Instead, use her experience as the basis for your advice and support.

✳ Pay attention to your daughter's criticisms of your parenting. Teenagers are bound to think we're doing something wrong. Above all, listen and think carefully about the merits of her arguments so that you can react more appropriately. Use this discussion as an opportunity for mutual assessment. We are not telling you to cave in when your daughter says everyone else's parents let them do something or that you are the meanest parent on earth. It does mean that sometimes it does pay to listen to what your daughter is saying and reconsider your positions.

＊ Don't assume that something is wrong if your daughter doesn't want to talk. Look for clues to depression, such as excessive sleeping (*far* more than normal), changing eating habits, not enjoying activities she usually takes pleasure in, and a drop in grades (see Appendix D: "Depression in Adolescent Girls").

＊ Know what resources are available if your child needs help—these include family members, friends, clergy, or mental health professionals. The most important thing is having the courage to ask others for help or guidance.

3. Be truthful and provide honest feedback when appropriate.

＊ Be an accurate mirror for your daughter and be truthful. Let her know when her behavior is not appropriate.

＊ Know and learn to like yourself. Understanding your own personal baggage is essential to determining what is important so you can transmit your values to your daughter. Daniel Siegel and Mary Hartzell write in *Parenting from the Inside Out* that the best predictor of a child's sense of self is how a parent feels about himself or herself. For example, if a mom criticizes her own body, her daughter may well have a more difficult time developing self-confidence.

＊ Be firm and truthful on matters involving fundamental values. Be flexible when possible. Being firm and flexible at the appropriate times gives you more credibility. Try to respond to your daughter consistently so she'll know what to expect from you.

✳ Be willing to compromise. When your daughter sees that you are willing to compromise, it gives you more authority. Besides, compromise shares the power with your daughter. You don't lose control when you compromise; you lose control when you are inconsistent and arbitrary. For example, one parent said, "Even though I couldn't concentrate on my homework with TV or music on, I saw that my daughter could. Why make a doctrine—an empty rule about something that may not be necessary. Don't buy trouble."

4. Allow your daughter to express a full range of emotions, including those that may be difficult for you to listen to or handle.

✳ Allow your daughter freedom of expression. Show your daughter that you accept her full range of emotions and that they are neither good nor bad. This will enable her to develop an authentic self, one that celebrates her uniqueness. While girls need to be respectful, they should be made to feel that all emotions are valid. Hopping hormones can mean abundant tears one moment and the big eye roll in the next.

✳ Teach your daughter that it's OK to express anger in an appropriate manner. Without an accepted outlet for aggression, she may submerge these difficult feelings and express her anger in a covert way, such as by bullying and gossiping. She may also internalize these feelings and turn them against herself, for example, through cutting and eating disorders. Both of these options are unhealthy for her psychological and emotional well-being.

✳ Teach her to understand that, for example, "I hate you, Mom!" may really mean "I feel angry when you don't let me do what my friends are allowed to do." When she is able to express herself in a more appropriate way, you can better tell her that you understand how she is feeling. Then you can calmly explain your position.

✳ Provide realistic feedback about emotional discomfort and how long it lasts. The instant culture in which our daughters live makes it difficult for them to be patient with real time. Teens expect their discomfort to be fixed as quickly as an instant message is transmitted.

5. Set and maintain appropriate boundaries.

✳ Be clear about your expectations for behavior.

✳ Convey your core values. Reflect on what is most important to you, and transmit these values clearly to your daughter. Be sure you are consistent, telling her and showing her through your own behavior what you value. If you say you value family time but are never home for dinner, the message will be diluted.

✳ Practice engaged detachment. Take a deep breath, step back, think about your core values, be reasonable about your goals, and know which issues you are willing to fight over and which ones you are willing to let go of. This approach provides you with the opportunity to state (and often restate) your values, rules, and fears, such as clarifying rules about smoking, drinking and drugs, driving, curfew, being home alone, computer use, and dating. Be clear about the consequences for breaking these rules.

✳ Based on your daughter's age, involve her in appropriate decision making about some of the rules. Her participation encourages a sense of investment and accountability because she feels some control over her life.

✳ Observe closely where your daughter spends her time and with whom. If done with reasonable boundaries, this concern can be presented as caring rather than as an attempt to control. One mom told us about her "worry rule": "My kids have tremendous freedom. They can go as long as I know where they are and they check in with me before I'm consumed with worry. This is not negotiable: if I don't know where they are and I try to reach them, they lose some freedom."

* Discuss the difference between healthy and dangerous risk taking. Healthy risk taking has a purpose. Adolescents use risk taking to help them develop their identities. Healthy risk taking is trying out a new sport that could be dangerous if not done correctly, such as skiing or scuba diving, or doing something that is scary, such as singing on stage or leaving home to attend a summer program. Unhealthy risk taking involves excessive use of alcohol and drugs, having unprotected sex, and walking home late at night alone.

* Don't worry about being your daughter's best friend at this stage of her life. Abdicating your authority confuses her and gives her too much control over the relationship.

* Place the computer in a visible, public place such as the family room, and set limits on Internet use. Talk with your daughter about online dangers. Enforce a list of "don'ts," including not giving out personal information and not completing personal profiles.

* Give your daughter sufficient privacy to allow her to develop her independent identity. Don't stand over her when she is on the telephone, and knock on her door before you enter her bedroom.

"Important sources of resistance to . . . negative cultural messages for adolescent girls include the following: a strong ethnic identity, close connections to family, learning positive messages about oneself, trusting oneself as a source of knowledge, speaking one's mind, participation in athletics, nontraditional sex typing, feminist ideas, and assertive female role models."
—AMERICAN PSYCHOLOGICAL ASSOCIATION TASK FORCE ON
  ADOLESCENT GIRLS: STRENGTHS AND STRESSES, "A New Look at
  Adolescent Girls"

6. Resist the urge to fix everything.

* Avoid doing everything for your daughter. When you overdo, you disable your daughter and erode her growing self-esteem. Doing for her puts you in the position of personal concierge, and this may render her permanently dependent and you permanently exhausted.

* Show your daughter that you love, respect, and have confidence in her. This is especially important when she makes mistakes or experiences failure. You cannot protect her from conflict, disappointments, frustrations, or mistakes. These experiences are inevitable and affirm her ability to cope with life's challenges (e.g., her ability to make new friends). Life is never perfect, and the best teacher is failure. This is the hardest thing to remember in parenting.

* Permit her to experience natural consequences, which teach personal responsibility and contribute to your daughter's self-esteem. Some natural consequences are acceptable; for example, being late for school may lead to detention, or forgetting to sign up for an activity will close her out of the one she may want. These consequences contribute to building personal responsibility.

* Accept the fact that mistakes and failure are inevitable. Through these experiences, your daughter will sharpen her problem-solving skills, learn to see life as it is, and develop tenacity and strength. At the same time, it is appropriate to create a safety net that provides her with a place where she can take risks and express her individuality.

7. Provide your daughter with alternatives to popular culture.

* Engage your daughter in honest discussions about popular culture, including the realities of what she sees on TV and in movies, reads in magazines, and hears in music.

* Counter the pop culture images of female physical perfection with an analysis of how they are used to market and sell goods and products. Let your daughter know that self-worth is defined by who she is and has less to do with physical appearance. This doesn't mean that she shouldn't strive to look her best, but, rather, that appearance is not the ultimate expression of self. Prevailing media power is such an overwhelming influence; we can't emphasize this message enough.

* Teach your daughter women's history and highlight positive role models so she will understand the context of her life and learn the lessons necessary to prepare for her future.

* Encourage and model healthy eating habits and exercise. Good lifestyle habits promote good health. Girls who participate in sports have more self-esteem than those who don't engage in athletics.

* Encourage girls to be more fluid with peer groups. Teach them to avoid being boxed in by a particular set of norms and standards just because they belong to one particular social group. This approach will enable them to explore a variety of interests and develop new skills.

8. Educate your daughter about her sexuality.

* Initiate frank and honest discussions about sexual behaviors and the risks that come with sexual freedom, including AIDS and other sexually transmitted diseases and pregnancy. Also discuss birth control options. With increased sexual freedom must come increased personal responsibility.

* Use everyday opportunities to talk about sexual behavior, rather than resorting to "the big talk." (It's a good idea to do this with most of the issues we address in this book—continual conversations about these ideas will be more effective than one major lecture.)

✳ Engage your daughter in conversations about the knowledge and skills she needs to protect herself in risky situations. For example, discuss the dangers of drinking and being with a boy who is under the influence of alcohol or drugs. Make sure she has contingency plans. One family told us that they keep taxi money in a drawer. Be available by phone; this is the best justification for teens to have a cell phone. Your daughter should never have an excuse for not calling.

✳ Explain to your daughter that sex is a mature act and that you expect her to avoid having early sexual experiences.

✳ Expect your daughter to demonstrate personal responsibility with regard to her health and safety. This is possible only with knowledge about sexuality. Behaving responsibly will enable a girl to make decisions about sexual relationships in a manner that maintains her self-respect. One mother told her daughter, "Don't do anything that you don't want to hear about in the school cafeteria the next day." It's also useful for girls to think not just about the cafeteria the next day, but also that sexual activities will be lifelong memories, and that they want them to be positive ones.

9. Begin early to nurture freedom from stereotypes and gender-specific expectations.

✳ Help your daughter to find her own voice. Give her the message that she doesn't always have to be a "nice" girl, "a pleaser," or compliant. She should be able to speak up and be her own advocate without fear of retribution because of her gender. It is through these experiences that she becomes her own person.

✳ Teach tolerance and respect for others; considering the feelings of other people helps to build empathy. Your most influential teaching will be by modeling these values yourself. Catch yourself if you find yourself making judgmental remarks about other people. Show your daughter that you are able to show respect for others who have ideas or ways different from yours. You provide the best antidote to sexism and prejudice.

* Watch how your daughter treats others. Provide feedback, both positive and negative, about whether your daughter is treating others with respect and consideration. Instant messaging is a new tool used to gossip and spread rumors. As much as possible, be aware of how your daughter uses this technology.

* Don't tolerate bullying or exclusionary behavior. Understand that in a millisecond your daughter can be the object of this kind of behavior. Your ignoring hurtful behavior perpetuates harassment and prejudice and indicates tacit approval.

* Support your daughter if she identifies herself as a lesbian. Listen to her carefully and with respect, and avoid dismissing her by suggesting that she's just going through a phase. Support from parents is essential if girls are going to be able to come through their teenage years intact. Gay and lesbian teens are often forced into isolation at a time when they need connection and support. Seek help from groups, such as PFLAG (Parents, Family and Friends of Lesbians and Gays), that can share their experience and provide insight. For girls, suggest groups such as SMYAL (Sexual Minority Youth Assistance League) for support.

10. Stay involved with your daughter's education all the way through school.

* Maintain high expectations for your daughter's performance in school. Encourage your daughter to set her own standards. There is no greater motivator than success, and success builds self-confidence.

* Know the classes your daughter is taking and how they contribute to her preparation for the future. If your daughter is reticent about taking more challenging courses, find out if her reticence can be addressed with support. Talk with her school counselor and see if tutoring would help your daughter feel more comfortable taking the class.

* Encourage your daughter to stretch herself, including trying academic subjects that are considered nontraditional to her gender, such as math and science. Make sure that career counselors are giving her the same message and that her teachers are supporting her. Be aware that girls may avoid tough classes in favor of receiving higher grades in easier subjects; let them know this is not the way to achieve true success.

* Make sure that girls (especially in middle school) are not in a position to think they have to choose between friends and performance. Praise your daughter when she achieves in school. Tell her that if her friends make her feel bad when she chooses to study rather than hang out, they may not be the best friends for her. This is an important life lesson.

* Treat bullying behavior seriously. Don't dismiss or trivialize hurtful or bullying behavior with the platitude, "girls will be girls," which serves only to encourage this type of behavior.

* Teach your daughter how to defend herself against being victimized. If other kids make fun of your daughter, strategize with her to empower and protect her from feeling like a victim. Identifying and naming this behavior gives girls a sense of empowerment. For example, if your daughter expresses anger or sadness because she is being picked on or teased, help her to identify this behavior as bullying or harassment. This sense of power may give her the courage to go to the appropriate authorities at school and get help. You could also role-play with your daughter about what to say to the bullies. If you become aware that your daughter is a bully, help her to understand how being targeted by a bully feels, and praise her for more appropriate behavior.

* Be prepared to intervene in school if your daughter shows signs of distress, but be aware of the reality of teen social dynamics, most especially your daughter's fears and emotions.

* Encourage participation in sports and other extracurricular activities. Involvement in these activities is a great way to develop self-confidence. By participating in competitive sports, girls learn to respond positively to competition, to be part of a team, to be more goal-oriented, to have integrity by learning to make a commitment and keep it, to gain opportunities to feel courageous, and, with sports, to have a better body image. These characteristics affect all other parts of girls' lives.

* Don't buy into the negative press that the gains girls have made in education are achieved at the expense of boys. Pitting boys against girls is an unnecessary lose-lose situation. Girls and boys deserve to have equal opportunities.

11. Give your daughter the skills to find balance in her future life.

* Help your daughter to set goals. Discuss the choices and challenges of her future life, including balancing family and work. Be candid about the challenges, and share some of the strategies that have worked for you. Avoid giving your daughter the message that she needs to be a superwoman.

* Help her to understand that with choices come both responsibilities and compromises. For a generation that is not satisfied by doing with less, this is a critical lesson. Children may feel entitled and want everything immediately. This entitlement starts early. One mother lov-

ingly called her daughter "Instant Isabel," because the moment she identifies a need, she can't tolerate waiting for it to be met.

* Advise your daughter not to lose herself in a relationship. Girls should not have to sacrifice their needs, passions, or ambitions to have a relationship. They can be more than caretakers. Relationships work better when both parties have their needs met.

* Be tolerant of your daughter's choices, which may be different from the ones you might make.

* Teach your daughter money-management skills.

12. Encourage your daughter to develop a meaningful relationship with her dad.

* Provide opportunities for dads and daughters to spend time together. Dads help their daughters to achieve, engage in activities non-traditional to their gender, and provide a model for adult relationships with males. Dads give them the courage to do something that they may be hesitant to try.

* Don't treat your daughter like a "princess," because, as Harriet Lerner writes in *The Dance of Connection*, "Being an idealized child carries a high price tag. It interferes with self-esteem, which requires us to have an objective view of our strengths and limitations. . . . Idealization is seductive. But . . . a pedestal, like a prison, is a small place to navigate."

* Encourage daughters to "de-princess" themselves by developing realistic relationships with their dads that incorporate both competence and acceptance. Realistic expectations enable girls to maintain more accurate views of themselves. Lerner adds that this perspective is invaluable for developing healthy relationships with boys because it

creates a more realistic expectation of the other person and limits the destructive expectations that come from a sense of entitlement.

13. Provide positive opportunities for connection. Connection is what sustains us.

* Connection to self, family, and community serves as an anchor for girls during these turbulent years.

* Spend time with your daughter, even when she fights it. Maintain the tradition of family dinners as much as possible. It's just as important to spend time with her as a teenager as it was when she was a child. This involvement is essential to maintaining connection and developing a positive long-term parent-child relationship.

* Stay in touch with your daughter. Your relationship can help to mitigate her involvement with risky behavior.

* Create a teen-friendly house where kids feel comfortable. A good way to learn about your daughter is to get to know her friends.

* Support relationships with boys as friends. Don't assume that all male relationships are sexual. There are "mean" girls and "player" boys, but there are infinite opportunities for positive relationships and friendships with boys and girls.

* Teach your daughter the skills associated with personal responsibility, empathy, trust, and loyalty, all of which are critical for maintaining good friendships.

* Let her know that some friendships are worth the investment, while others are not. Discuss the importance of having friends who genuinely make her feel good about herself and are trustworthy and loyal. Authentic friendships give her permission to be herself.

✳ Encourage relationships with other adults who care about your daughter. It's important for girls to relate to and trust other adults. Sometimes it's easier for them to talk to adults who are not their parents. Become friends with the parents of your daughter's friends. They often can provide a perspective with which you would feel comfortable, and your daughter may find it easier to listen to them. And, you may find out what a great kid your daughter is when she automatically clears the table at their house!

✳ Above all else, maintain a sense of perspective and humor.

Life with teenage girls often feels precarious, because their energy is so powerful and the risks that they face are so great. They confront the challenges of drugs and alcohol, early sexual experiences, and the power of peer groups and the media. These extremely strong influences explain why parents often feel overwhelmed. As parents, you have no choice but to meet these challenges. You must stay involved. You provide the perspective that can transform your daughter's life from one of distorted images into a triumph of self-confidence, high expectations, and resilience.

You are your daughter's most dependable and enduring role model. Remember that children are resilient and good parents are not perfect. Stay close, stay connected, and trust your instincts about what is best for your daughter. Regardless of what she may say, she looks to you for assurance.

IT'S ABOUT THAT TIME

Girls and Boys Together

"For 10 years, the Ms. Foundation encouraged Americans to 'take our daughters to work.' More than 70 million did just that, and 40% were men. That got Ms. to thinking, and now it has launched Take Our Daughters and Sons to Work Day. Activities are also designed to encourage girls and boys to think about how to balance work with family life when they have their own children. The kids may even have some ideas for the companies who'll one day employ them."

—Reported by LYRIC WALLWORK WINIK,
in *Parade* magazine

Children's development is strongly influenced by the expectations and behaviors of their parents and other adult role models. It is important for these adults to behave in ways that have the most positive effect on a child's development. To be a parent rather than a friend, you have to establish appropriate boundaries while maintaining connection.

Most important, we believe you must listen to what your children are saying. For girls, this means listening through the noise to decipher what they are really telling you; for boys, this means learning to pick up what are often brief and subtle clues and being available during the times they choose to come to you. To parent effectively, you must be clear about your core values and convey them to your children. Self-knowledge and self-reflection are a critical part of parenting. Self-discovery is a lifelong process.

In making decisions, you have to remember that your children have been on earth for only a relatively short time, so they have only that much knowledge; no matter how sophisticated they are or how much of the world they've seen, that's all they have the capacity to know. You have more years of experience, so you are expected to have some wisdom and the capability to help guide your children in a positive direction. The number of years that you have been on this earth counts for something.

Parenting is not about friendship, at least during this stage. You can't parent effectively if you abdicate your authority and allow your children to control the relationship. Conventional wisdom speaks volumes about the importance of spending time with your children when they are young. We believe it is at least as important to be present and involved during the teen years. While your children may want you to disappear or put a bag over your head and not ask any questions, now is a critical time to be involved. Your involvement is essential to maintain connection and to support your teenagers' evolution into adulthood. This interaction also helps to sustain your relationships with your children.

For girls, you have to be careful not to misread the drama that often comes with being a teenager. You need to ask: "Are you upset at me, or are you upset about something that happened with your friends?" "Are you going to Julie's tonight, or are you going to the party that I heard about?" "Will there be drinking there?" And even if they say no, that doesn't necessarily mean no, especially when it's an event or activity that they really want to participate in. Objective coaching and critical questions are essential to get to the bottom of the issue. Once again, this is your chance to state your values, fears, and rules.

For boys, who tend to be less open and answer everything with, "No problem" or "I'm fine," you have to be able to read their clues and then ask a few questions at a time and be satisfied as well as able to make decisions based on less information. You have to be ready to seize the moment when he comes to you, because, as one parent said, "It may not come again for days." It's in these individual moments that you and your children develop a process for maintaining connection.

Because human beings are hardwired to connect, you should recognize that you have the ability to create an environment for your children that can increase their well-being substantially. George Will writes in the *Washington Post* that, according to a recent study aptly titled "Hardwired to Connect," the developing brain of a child can protect him or her from vulnerabilities by promoting opportunities for connection, which creates resiliency. The "family is the most basic authoritative community . . . the most crucial [for developing social connectedness]. A child's relational context, which is just another way of saying connection, is what sustains and protects them."

Beyond Stereotypes

From pink and blue tags in hospitals to advertisements and articles about beauty care, cosmetics, fashion, dating; rap songs; ESPN; and video games such as Madden 2004, cultural messages are clear about what it means to be a boy or a girl in our society. Even though, "It has become politically correct for some hospitals and parents to adopt gender-neutral colors such as yellow or white for newborns, . . . the significance of blue and pink as a permanent symbol of gender remains," reports Jim Nieken in "Boys Are Better Than Girls: Adolescent Gender Socialization in North America." These perceptions about females and males have widespread effects on the quality of life for teenagers.

Children are born free of cultural bias. They learn the language of culture from their parents, teachers, and the media through socialization. Socialization defines the differences between women and men in such areas as thinking patterns, needs, and communication styles. Many of the stereotypes of masculinity and femininity have been constructed by society, and we too frequently rely on them when we ascribe meaning to certain behaviors, characteristics, and attitudes.

Stereotypes confront us daily, promoting assumptions that strong boys are assertive while strong girls are aggressive. Competitive boys are ambitious; competitive girls are dominant and too pushy. If adolescence is a time of conformity, such expectations have the effect of limiting boys' and girls' interests, skills, behavior, and pursuits. Stereotyping is insidious because it creates unnecessary and harmful losses. Both boys and girls are asked to give up some part of themselves. We want to limit the losses and expand the way our children look at and approach the world, rather than confine their world to a particular view.

Few behaviors, characteristics, or attitudes are actually biological or physiological; few can be linked specifically to the fact that a person is male or female, according to Alisa J. McClure in "Wimpy Boys and Macho Girls: Gender Equity at the Crossroads." While we are all born with a clearly defined biology that identifies us as either male or female, we are not born with a handbook describing how to be a boy or a girl. Culture provides us with a road map.

Schools and the media compete with parents to be the primary influences on American socialization of children. Schools place children in contact with their peers, who have great influence on social perceptions and conduct. Movies, television, and music provide our children box seats to the media's fabricated view about cultural values, offering nonstop messages to every family's home. These powerful influences notwithstanding, we believe you are your children's first and most important teachers.

The process of socialization is not without compromise. Girls are supposed to be thin and pretty, and boys are not allowed to cry. These conventions have their genesis in anthropology. Historically, men in Western culture have been expected to center their lives on publicly visible accomplishments (for example, by being providers and leaders). Women have been expected to center their lives on relationships and more personal accomplishments (for example, as caretakers and home-makers). As a result, many girls are socialized to view their identities as being tied exclusively to relationships. While these social norms may have been helpful to society at one time, they don't serve the same purpose today.

We believe that each gender can be free from the constraints of cultural straitjackets only when young women and young men break out of strict cultural stereotypes. One gender frees the other. Girls do not grow or benefit at the expense of boys, and boys do not grow at the expense of girls. Without the pressure to "prove" their manhood or womanhood, boys and girls can grow in ways that are natural and comfortable for them as individuals, rather than in reaction to pre-conceived ways of being.

The image that comes to mind is a plant placed in a sunny window with access to plenty of light. Rather than bending and curving to search for their light source in a partially lit window, girls and boys can be nurtured to grow to their full potential. We have written *Why Girls Talk* and *Why Boys Don't Talk* to provide you with a road map as you navigate the challenges of parenting teenagers.

Empowering Girls

Self-sufficiency for girls includes being, as one mother described, "sturdy" or strong, having strength of character, being able to advocate for themselves, developing a positive self-image, feeling confident about what they know and feel, and choosing friends who bring out

"Dr. Barbara Staggers shares: 'With all the kids I know who make it, there's one thing in common: individual contact with an adult who cared and kept hanging in there.'"
—DOUGLAS FOSTER, "The Disease Is Adolescence"

the best in them. Girls should be comfortable with their appearance and put concerns about physical beauty into a healthy perspective. We want them to be able to be themselves, speak their mind, and have friends but not subjugate or lose their voice to belong to a particular peer group. When they have other selves to draw on (spheres of competence), they are able to define themselves not only by their group status but also as individuals who happen to be part of a group. This enables girls to individualize somewhat during their teenage years. These qualities will counteract, as one mother described, "waiting to see what the response is going to be from other people, which cuts them off from their authentic selves, rather than feeling good about themselves for what they do."

Freedom of expression allows girls to develop an authentic self, one that celebrates their uniqueness. While enhancing their individuality, we want girls to continue to experience the joy of connection. These qualities of authenticity and connection form the building blocks for becoming a resilient adult. Maturity doesn't happen all at once; it is a process over time and is accomplished in incremental steps. This process requires your support and guidance to help make it go as well as possible.

Once we give girls the freedom to make choices without the constraining girdle of society that dictates appropriate behavior for them, we give them permission to make mistakes and explore new territory. We believe that girls will take more risks, and they will go after what they want with more confidence. With change comes both opportunity and challenge. In an interview with author Laura Sessions Stepp, she discusses a goal for girls: "We have to teach girls that sometimes power comes in holding back, not giving everything. It comes in knowing who you are as a person and valuing that and not giving it up so easily. That's power. I think we need to set boundaries for girls. We need to help them find things about themselves that they value and stress to them how precious those things are, and they're not something that you give away. . . ."

Having a voice and being herself give a girl the freedom to choose different and multiple social roles, which can include nurturer, athlete, friend, mother, companion, leader, and worker. You should expect that new freedom and independence require a reconceptualization of what you may have believed to be true for girls. With the new options available to girls, we should anticipate that they will make mistakes and experience failure, and we need to share this reality with our daughters. It isn't that girls haven't always made mistakes, but, today, for many of us, the options and risks seem unfamiliar.

You have to initiate conversations with your children about the issues they face every day. From our focus groups and national surveys, we have learned that teens want to talk to adults about these real-life issues. If you wait for your kids to come to you, your children could be at risk, and you will miss the opportunity to guide them. By failing to initiate conversations about risk behaviors, you gamble with your children's safety and well-being. For example, when we keep our heads in the sand about issues such as sexual behavior, we put our children at risk for unsafe sex. While it may be tough for you to talk and listen, talking and listening are certainly safer than unsafe sex!

With greater sexual freedom must come increased personal responsibility. Girls should be able to enjoy a sexual relationship on their own terms. The current environment, which considers desire more acceptable, should not require girls to do more than they want to do. You have so little control of your daughter's sexual images; it's not surprising that girls appear to be sexual before they understand how others may interpret their conduct. For your daughter to protect herself from the onslaught of sexualization, she needs to have a good sense of who she is. A strong self-concept will help her to take care of herself sexually and to set appropriate boundaries.

You need to be tuned into the differences between dangerous and healthy risk taking, because not all risk taking is bad. Some risks are worth taking for teenagers to develop self-esteem and learn how to manage consequences. Healthy risks include stretching themselves academically, trying out for the school play, or leaving home to experience a different culture. Only through taking risks can they learn how to cope with disappointment.

Even though all parents were once teenagers, most of us seem to forget (or choose to forget!) what this period of development is like. We forget that, developmentally, teens are supposed to make mistakes. As one 14-year-old girl said, "We're teenagers; that's what we do. We make stupid mistakes often and don't know why we made them." Teenage risk is scary, but some risk taking is a developmental necessity. Even with the best parenting, you can't protect your children from being disliked, teased, and tempted by risky or dangerous choices. We worry that, as parents, if we encourage their independence we may inadvertently place our children at risk.

There are risks in life from which you can't protect your children, no matter how many safeguards you put in place. These include driving cars (a legitimate fear) and going to parties (why we can't sleep until they get home) or learning a new sport, whether it's snowboarding or rock climbing. While you can't prevent them from experiencing failure, you can strengthen their judgment and sense of self by discussing and allowing them to experience consequences. The problem today is that our children live in a much more dangerous world than we did at their age. Because the world feels more threatening, we are more reluctant as parents to let our children go, and there are more factors to consider with every decision and every act. It's not that we don't want them to have experiences, we just have to work harder at teaching them to use good judgment.

You aren't going to prevent them from taking risks, but judgment is about mitigating risks, not eliminating them. You have to ask the hard questions so that your children can learn for themselves to lessen the risks and to manage their choices successfully. They can often be hard to approach, so you and other adults in their lives have to initiate difficult conversations and keep the lines of communication open.

Your job as a parent, along with other caring adults, is to create a safe environment for girls to express their individuality and to try out new things. This is why we feel it's so important for girls to build their own personal compass—identifying what their core values are and being able to both access and act on them. Establishing a personal compass also allows girls to find their way back to parents who love them unconditionally.

Mixed Signals

This period for parents and girls is truly a time of trial and error. Because parents also have a learning curve, they sometimes give their daughters mixed messages. The truth is that we don't have all the answers and we are not immune to the world around us. Unconditional love helps to mitigate the inevitable mistakes we all make as parents. When you are raising teenagers and are aware of the mixed messages and complicated social world they face, you can be more forgiving of their mistakes and build understanding and honesty between yourself and your children.

Many parents said that they wanted their daughters to be both individuals and well liked and popular. This is not a problem until you tell your daughter to keep her mouth shut so that her friends will like her better. Karen, a 15-year-old, said, "My parents tell me that I shouldn't express myself with such strong convictions because it sounds too harsh. My mom tells me to be softer, and I don't do that well because she also tells me to stick by my guns. So what's up?" Parents do something similar to boys when we want our sons to be well-rounded yet worry that if they like art or drama too much, others will consider them soft.

Parents say, "My daughter will talk more. And my son, I probably let him be a little more silent because I just figure that's the way boys are." One mother told us that when her son, Darren, would refuse to discuss his social life, she dropped the topic. He would put the palm of his hand in the air to let her know to stop probing, and she knew immediately that the conversation was over. However, two years earlier she had constantly pressed her daughter, Laurie, for details about the boys in her life, even when Laurie was reluctant to talk. This mom assumed that Laurie's hesitation meant that something must be wrong and that Darren somehow had an intrinsic right to his privacy. We consistently respect our sons' boundaries even as we often trample over our daughters'.

It's hard not to get caught up in the drama of your daughter's life. The noise of teen drama is pervasive. As parents we must be mindful of the distinction between what girls say and what they really mean. Connection (to self-knowledge, families, and communities) serves as the anchor, while all this teen-girl drama surrounds us. Connection is the life jacket that keeps girls afloat during these turbulent years.

Boys and Girls at the Crossroads

It is "important for boys and girls to learn to work and play together in a friendly, respectful manner, outside the box of gender or cliques or favorite friend status," say Tamara Grogan and Lynn Bechtel in "Improving Gender Relationships in School." "And students can learn how to do this in the context of daily classroom life, classroom by classroom, teacher by teacher." These friendships enable girls and boys to have a better understanding of each other. As one father said, "They will know each other better. Therefore, adult relationships will be stronger."

Contrary to popular opinion, boys are interested in spending more time getting to know girls in a nonsexual way. Boys are often more comfortable telling their innermost feelings to girls. One 16-year-old boy said, "One of the reasons I would hold back in going into a relationship with a girl*friend* is that if something happens, if we break up, I might also lose her friendship."

The mother of a 14-year-old son and twin 17-year-old daughters said, "I think, particularly, boys who grow up with sisters have tremendous respect for girls. They see girls putting away their soccer cleats, studying for the AP tests, and highlighting their hair. I think that they've seen firsthand girls who achieve, girls who assert themselves, and girls who are not afraid to speak their minds."

Another parent added, "I also think that both boys and girls are beginning to see more equitable relationships between their own parents and the benefits of this kind of marriage. I'm certain that my son is very clear that my job allowed my husband the freedom to change his job when he was so unhappy. So kids today can see the advantages of a couple who work together for the family, rather than a husband who is dominant and a wife who is submissive."

Times change. While teenagers today certainly engage in dating and intimate relationships, for the most part, these are different from the ones we experienced. Teens tend to hang out in groups, with boys and girls together. It is not uncommon for girls to go to homecoming dances with other girls, rather than pairing off. Boys also go with groups of friends. They may "hook up" with each other, but they are also careful to protect their boy-girl friendships.

Boys are also struggling with balance—how to be independent and stay connected in a world that is increasingly asking them to be both. For boys, our need to enshrine independence has been at war with the basic human need for love, support, and emotional encouragement. Male maturity is not shamed or emasculated by having a parent or parents who want their son to remain competent and close. One parent observed, "I'm interested in how much more relational girls are than guys, and my sense is that guys long for relationships. They just don't know how to achieve them."

Through their experience as friends, teenagers are learning to recognize and combat gender bias and to treat each other equally and with respect, regardless of gender. In her book *The Difference: Growing Up Female in America*, Judy Mann observes, "For men and boys, the journey is away from dominance. For girls and women, the journey is toward empowerment. For both, the prize is the true joy that is found in relationships based on equality."

Leaving a Legacy

Boys and girls have much to learn from one another. Boys can learn how to be relational, how to be connected in a way that provides them with the nurturing that connection traditionally has provided for girls and women. From boys, girls can learn to speak out, to say what's on their minds without equivocation, to demand to be heard, and to avoid a tailspin after a disagreement or an insult. Girls can learn how

---

WHAT WOULD LIFE BE LIKE?

Ask your daughter, "What do you think your life would be like if you woke up tomorrow morning as a boy?" Ask her to think about some of these questions:

1. How might the way you think about your appearance be affected?
2. What activities might you do? At work? At home? In the community?
3. What might be the same in your behavior? What might be different?
4. How might others (strangers, family members, colleagues, and friends) treat you differently?
5. What does looking at the life of a boy show you about how you feel about being a girl?

---

to move on and put everyday aggravations into perspective. You can help to foster the best qualities in both boys and girls.

We realize that a girl's tendency to seek connection often creates a constant buzz in our homes, including what many parents describe as "worry-talk, drama, and reactive" behavior. At the same time, this emphasis on relationship is also valuable and helps us to better understand ourselves. In our meetings with girls and parents during the course of writing this book, we have been reminded continually of the joy, complexity, and energy that girls bring to a family.

Love and accept her for who she is, not for who you think she should be or for what she does. Society takes care of that. It is very important to communicate this to girls because they are bombarded with so many mixed messages, including that girls should be both assertive and compliant; that looks aren't important and appearance is everything; and that girls can do anything, but glass ceilings still exist. Your acceptance of a real girl—one who struggles with all of these conflicts—supports her, giving her the ammunition to fight mixed messages and thrive. The connection between you and your daughter is a powerful catalyst for growth. The teenage years are a period of tremendous growth for both of you. Don't forget to take the time to enjoy your daughter and marvel at the changes taking place in her before your very eyes.

"I long to put the experience of fifty years at once into your young lives, to give you at once the key to that treasure chamber every gem of which has cost me tears, struggles, and prayers, but you must work for these inward treasures yourselves."

—HARRIET BEECHER STOWE, in a letter to her twin daughters

APPENDIX A

POSITIVE PARENTING

The Law of Return

"One good parent is worth 1,000 schoolmasters."

—Chinese proverb

The purpose of this parent brief is to present 13 principles of positive parenting:

1. Parenting is a process. You never arrive with all the skills that you need.
2. Parents are not trained to be parents; kids are not trained to be kids. Kids train parents; parents train kids.
3. It is more challenging to be a parent than to function in your job.
4. Parenting is a journey, not a destination.
5. Parents are the most significant influence in a child's life.

6. A parent is the greatest teacher a child will ever have. A parent and child certainly have the longest teaching relationship ever known.
7. It is not a question of whether a parent is a teacher or not; it's a question of what is taught. Parents teach kids a whole language before they go to school.
8. What you need to learn, you teach your child best.
9. Parent modeling that includes the unspoken as well as the spoken word is the most powerful force in shaping a child's life.
10. How you spend your time and money tells your kids what you value, regardless of what you say.
11. Successful parenting is predictable, reliable, and consistent.
12. There's a difference between an investment that sounds good and a sound investment. There's no greater investment in life than children.
13. Parents who praise each of their children at least twice a day maintain a positive relationship regardless of the problems they encounter.

Developed by the Mid-Atlantic Equity Center, Chevy Chase, MD: 1998.

APPENDIX B

Focus Group
Interview Guide

Adolescents

---

1. Are you glad that you are a girl? Why? Can you identify particular traits about girls that you are happy to have?
2. Do people treat you differently because you are a girl? Teachers? Parents? If you have a brother, is there a difference in how your parents treat him?
3. Do people treat you differently because of your race, culture, or ethnicity? If so, how does it make you feel? How do you respond?
4. How would you describe your friends? How are they like or unlike you? How do you choose your friends? Do they have to be cool? What is cool to you? What sort of things do you and your friends do together?
5. Do you and your friends fight? Do you ever talk about one friend to another? What kind of issue would create a falling out between you and a friend?

6. Have you ever ignored something that really hurt you because you were worried that it would ruin a friendship? Have you ever been really hurt by a friend or group of girls? If so, explain. Have you ever really hurt someone else?
7. Describe the power of your peer group.
8. Are you comfortable expressing anger to your friends, parents, or others? How do you express anger?
9. What is the easiest emotion to share—anger, sadness, happiness, love?
10. Do you have close friends of the opposite sex? What is it about these friends that you like? What do you see as the difference between a close friend of the opposite sex and a boyfriend?
11. What sorts of activities do you participate in (in or out of school)?
12. Describe your relationships with adults in your life.
13. If any of these relationships are not good, what would make them better?
14. Who are the most important adults in your life?
15. What happens to girls who stand out? Is this a good thing or a bad thing?
16. Is there anything you can do that sets you apart from other girls? Do you feel comfortable "tooting your own horn"? Do boys?
17. When you have a problem, what do you do? Do you seek advice from others? Who?
18. How do you feel about your body? Have you ever been on a diet? If so, when is the first time you ever restricted your food intake?
19. What is the message that your parents give you about your weight?
20. What are your aspirations regarding career and a future family?
21. How do you decide what is comfortable for you regarding sex? Is there pressure to do more or less than you want?
22. What do you think of when you hear the word *feminist*?
23. What are the differences between being a girl now and when your mom was growing up?

APPENDIX C

FOCUS GROUP INTERVIEW GUIDE

Parents

1. How would you describe your relationship with your daughter?
2. Have you noticed a time when your relationship with your daughter changed? If so, when did this occur?
3. What does it mean when we say "girls will be girls"?
4. How do you maintain boundaries with your daughter?
5. Did you notice any changes in your daughter's self-esteem as she entered adolescence?
6. What can you do to help build a competent girl? What kinds of strategies and experiences have worked for you?
7. How would you describe the media presentation of girls?
8. Who and what are you daughter's cultural icons?
9. What does she consider "beautiful"? How does she fit this model?
10. How do you mediate the influence of media and culture on your daughter's life?

11. What are the challenges of raising your daughter in a culture different from your own?
12. How influential is your daughter's peer group on her behavior, attitude, etc.?
13. Has she been the target of other girls' rejections or the instigator of rejection?
14. What kind of experience has your daughter had in school?
15. Do you have any conflict with your spouse in terms of raising your daughter?
16. What do you see as your daughter's greatest conflicts or struggles?
17. How does your daughter deal with anger and sadness? How does she handle conflict?
18. What happens to the nontraditional girl in today's society—school, culture, friends? How can you support her?
19. Do you think girls are in conflict over or torn between a traditional view of femininity and contemporary realities for what it is like to be a woman?
20. What are the critical issues between mothers and daughters during adolescence? Fathers and daughters?
21. What are some of the differences/similarities between raising daughters and sons?
22. What kinds of skills do you want your daughter to have in order to become a competent adult?
23. How do you work with your child to encourage her sense of well-being?
24. What are the two best pieces of advice that you would share with other parents of adolescent daughters?
25. What do you most enjoy about your daughter?

APPENDIX D

DEPRESSION IN ADOLESCENT GIRLS

Many of the tumultuous moods that we think are "normal" by-products of adolescence may be signs of depression. Depression symptoms should not be confused with or dismissed as adolescent mood swings.

When attempts at helping your daughter are ineffective, it is advisable to seek professional support, especially if the following symptoms persist for several weeks, become more severe, and/or lead to self-destructive thoughts or behavior. The following symptoms list has been developed by the National Institute of Mental Health:

* Persistent sad or "empty" mood, feeling hopeless
* Loss of enjoyment or interest in activities that provided pleasure in the past
* Changes in sleep habits such as insomnia or oversleeping
* Eating disturbances such as decreased appetite or overeating
* Difficulty in concentrating
* Physical aches such as headaches, stomach pain, and chronic pain that have no organic origin

* Low self-esteem
* Decreased energy

Risk factors for adolescent depression:

* Having a family member with depression
* Loss of an important family member or loved one to death
* Abuse or neglect
* Isolation, lack of support from trusted adults
* Harsh or judgmental parents with low tolerance for conflict or disagreements
* Overly permissive parents with few rules and regulations
* Family conflict regardless of parents' marital status

APPENDIX E

WARNING SIGNS OF
AN EATING DISORDER

There are several types of eating disorders, but all share some fundamental features:

* An extreme dissatisfaction with the body
* Body weight, size, or shape as primary measure of self-worth
* Feelings of guilt or depression after eating
* A tendency to isolate, to withdraw from friends and family
* Preoccupation with weight, food, calories, fat or carbohydrate grams, and diet

For bulimia nervosa, also look for the following:

* Periods of uncontrolled eating, or binges
* Self-induced vomiting or use of laxatives
* Excessive exercise, often used to "undo" the last eating episode

For binge eating disorder, also look for the following:

* Periods of uncontrolled eating, or binges
* Eating often when not hungry
* Eating until uncomfortably full

For anorexia nervosa, also look for the following:

* Dramatic weight loss
* Feeling fat despite dramatic weight loss
* Intense fear of fat
* Excessive exercise
* Odd food rituals such as counting bites, cutting food into tiny pieces, etc.
* Loss of menstrual periods, fainting, or irregular pulse

A Note About Dieting

Many eating disorders begin as a diet. Going on a diet is often the gateway to a full-blown eating disorder, both because it introduces unhealthy ideas about food and because it fosters excessive focus on the body. Popular culture is overflowing with dangerous misinformation about nutrition and the body, and nearly all of it can contribute to the development of eating-disordered beliefs and behaviors. If your daughter is dieting, using diet pills or diuretics, or eating under food rules such as "no carbohydrates" or "no eating after 5:00 P.M.," she is at risk.

If You Feel Concerned That Your Daughter Is "Fat" or "Getting Fat"

It is normal for preadolescents and adolescents to accumulate fat; the body is just storing up for the tremendous amount of energy it will need to physically develop into adulthood. This is most often a temporary state and should not be interfered with through diets or extra exercise. It is also important to remember that when transitioning from a girl's body to a woman's body, we gain more fat. This is a biological reality that is made more difficult by a society that fears even normal amounts of fat.

Despite what the diet industry tells us, each of us has a set body weight that is predetermined; we can do very little to change it. It is why diets never bring lasting weight loss and why some people spend their entire lives fighting those "last few pounds." Look at both sides of her biological family to get a sense of what her set body type might be. If she is bigger or heavier than she wishes, she may need support in learning to accept her natural body in a culture that overvalues the underweight look. Remember that beginning a diet can set her up for a demoralizing, lifelong, and—most important—losing battle. As long as your child is reasonably active and making thoughtful nutritional choices most of the time, it is unlikely that you need to worry. However, if your child is inactive or making poor food choices, she is at risk for obesity and other health problems. If you are concerned, it may be helpful to go to a nutritionist together to get guidance in making these lifestyle changes.

Eating disorders can be deadly, and over time they usually get worse and more difficult to treat. But when recognized early and with proper treatment, there is an excellent chance for recovery. If your child is showing any warning signs, it is important that you seek professional help as soon as possible. When looking for treatment, be sure that both the therapist and the nutritionist have had special training in treating eating disorders; don't be afraid to ask.

Kimberly Lawrence Kol, Psy.D.,
Clinical Psychologist/Eating Disorder Specialist

Resources

National Eating Disorders Association
Information and Referral Helpline: 1-800-931-2237
www.nationaleatingdisorders.org

Gurze Books (specializing in eating disorders publications
and education)
1-800-756-7533
www.gurze.com

References

Chapter 1

Brown, L., and C. Gilligan. *Meeting at the Crossroads: Women's Psychology and Girls' Development*. New York: Ballantine Books, 1993.

Chesler, P. *Woman's Inhumanity to Woman*. New York: Thunder's Mouth Press/Nation Books, 2001, 63, 92, 93, 95, 97.

Deak, J. *Girls Will Be Girls*. New York: Hyperion, 2002, 14, 96.

Garbarino, J., and E. deLara. "Words Can Hurt Forever." *Educational Leadership*, 60 no. 6 (March 2003): 18–21.

James, D. W., and G. Partee. *No More Islands: Family Involvement in 27 School and Youth Programs*. Washington, DC: American Youth Policy Forum, 2003.

Mann, J. *The Difference: Growing Up Female in America*. New York: Warner Books, 1994, 275.

Miller, J. B. *Toward a New Psychology of Women*. Boston: Beacon Press, 1976, 83.

Pipher, M. *Raising Ophelia: Saving the Lives of Adolescent Girls*. New York: Rimm, Ballantine Books, 1994, 292.

Shaffer, S., and L. Gordon. *Why Boys Don't Talk—and Why It Matters: A Parent's Survival Guide to Connecting with Your Teen*. New York: McGraw-Hill, 2005.

Simmons, R. *Odd Girl Out: The Hidden Culture of Aggression in Girls*. New York: Harcourt, 2002.

Wiltz, T. "Louise Erdrich: The Latest Installment." *Washington Post*, March 2, 2003, F1–F2.

Wiseman, R. *Queen Bees and Wannabes: Helping Your Daughter Survive Cliques, Gossip, Boyfriends, and Other Realities of Adolescence*. New York: Crown Publishing Group, 2003.

Chapter 2

AAUW Educational Foundation. *Girls in the Middle: Working to Succeed in School*. Washington, DC: AAUW Educational Foundation, 1996.

Bellafante, G. "Young and Chubby: What's Heavy About That?" *New York Times*, January 26, 2003, sec. 9, 1–2.

Brown, J. "Trash Mags with Training Wheels." Salon.com. www.about-face.org/r/press/salon091001.shtml (accessed July 29, 2003).

"The Facts About Figures." *People* (June 3, 1996): 71.

"Feminism and Adolescent Girls." www.angelfire.com/realm2/my_individuation/feminism.html (accessed May 23, 2003).

Giedrys, S. "Creating a Curriculum to Help Girls Battle Eating Disorders: Harvard Eating Disorder Center Strives to Raise Awareness of 'Weightism' in Our Culture." Harvard University Gazette. www.news.harvard.edu/gazette/1999/02.11/eating.html (accessed August 7, 2003).

Lamb, S. *The Secret Lives of Girls: What Good Girls Really Do—Sex Play, Aggression, and Their Guilt*. New York: The Free Press, 2001.

Mazzerella, S., and N. Pecora. *Growing Up Girls: Popular Culture and the Construction of Identity*. New York: Peter Lang, 1999, 211.

The Riverdeep Current. Teaching the News. "The Beauty Within." www.river deep.net/current/2002/05/050602t_beauty.jhtml (accessed June 14, 2003).

Rogers, M. *Barbie Culture.* Thousand Oaks, CA: Sage Publications, 2000.

Ryan, J. "Overestimating the Fidget Factor." *San Francisco Chronicle,* February 16, 2003, D1.

Salisbury, L. *Reflections of Girls in the Media: A Two-Part Study on Gender and Media.* Children Now. www.childrennow.org/media/mc97/ReflectSummary.cfm (accessed May 15, 2003).

"Self-Esteem and Young Women." Office of Juvenile Justice and Delinquency Prevention. www.ojjdp.ncjrs.org/pubs/gender/treat-2.html (accessed June 13, 2003).

"Statistics: How Many People Have Eating Disorders?" Anorexia Nervosa and Related Eating Disorders, Inc. (ANRED). www.anred.com/stats.html (accessed June 16, 2004).

Strauss, R. S. "The Facts." Independent Television Service. www.itvs.org/girlsinamerica/findings.html (accessed September 7, 2003).

Waterhouse, D. *Like Mother, Like Daughter: How Women Are Influenced by Their Mother's Relationship with Food and How to Break the Pattern.* New York: Hyperion, 1997, 95.

Wolf, N. "Hunger." In *Feminist Perspectives on Eating Disorders,* ed. P. Fallow, M. A. Katzman, and S. C. Wooley. New York: Guilford Press, 1994.

Chapter 3

"Alcohol Use Among Girls." U.S. Department of Health and Human Services and SAMHSA's National Clearinghouse for Alcohol and Drug Information. www.ncadi.samhsa.gov/govpubs/rp0993 (accessed April 1, 2003).

American Academy of Child and Adolescent Psychiatry. "Teen Suicide." www .aacap.org/publications/factsfam/suicide.htm (accessed November 1998).

American Association of University Women (AAUW). *Gender Gaps: Where Schools Still Fail Our Children.* Washington, DC: AAUW Educational Foundation, 1998.

Brown, L., and C. Gilligan. *Meeting at the Crossroads: Women's Psychology and Girls' Development.* New York: Ballantine Books, 1993.

Brumberg, J. *The Body Project.* New York: Random House, 1997.

Carlson, L. "Five Middle Schools Launch Program to Deal with Depression." *Gazette Community News,* March 12, 2002, A9.

Carnegie Council on Adolescent Development, Study on Self-Esteem, 2002.

Clinton, H. R. "Parenting a Teen . . ." *Newsweek* (May 8, 2000): 75.

Deak, J. *Girls Will Be Girls.* New York: Hyperion, 2002, 5, 17.

Debold, E. "Helping Girls Survive the Middle Grades." *Principal* 74 (January 3, 1995): 22–24.

Denizet-Lewis, B. "Friends, Friends with Benefits, and the Benefits of the Local Mall." *New York Times Magazine* (May 30, 2004): 33.

Edwards, E. "Middle Schoolers, Letting Their Fingers Do the Talking." *Washington Post,* May 14, 2003, C1.

Erikson, E. *Insight and Responsibility.* New York: W. W. Norton, 1964.

"The Formative Years: Pathways to Substance Abuse Among Girls and Young Women Ages 8–22." National Center on Addiction and Substance Abuse at Columbia University (CASA). www.casacolumbia.org/pdshopprov/shop/item.asp?itemid=13 (accessed September 10, 2004).

Giedd, J. N. "Brain Imaging of Children." Washington, DC: White House Conference on Teenagers, May 2, 2000.

Gilligan, C. *In a Different Voice.* Cambridge, MA: Harvard University Press, 1982.

Horsburgh, S., and J. Fowler. "A Survivor's Tale: Bouncing Back from Despair." *People* (September 15, 2003): 160.

Hutchinson, M. K., and T. M. Cooney. "Patterns of Parent-Teen Sexual Risk Communication: Implications for Intervention." *Family Relations* 47 (1998): 185–194.

Kates, J. "Angry Girls Use Friendship as a Weapon." www.girlscircle.com/article_gandm.html (accessed April 5, 2003).

Kohlberg, L. *The Philosophy of Moral Development.* San Francisco, CA: Harper and Row, 1981.

Lamb, S. *The Secret Lives of Girls: What Good Girls Really Do—Sex Play, Aggression, and Their Guilt.* New York: The Free Press, 2001, 147.

Miller, B. C. *Families Matter: A Research Synthesis of Family Influences on Adolescent Pregnancy.* Washington, DC: National Campaign to Prevent Teen Pregnancy, 1998.

Mundy, L. "Sex Sensibility." *Washington Post Magazine* (July 16, 2000): 30.

National Institute on Alcohol Abuse and Alcoholism (NIAAA). *Make a Difference: Talk to Your Child About Alcohol.* Bethesda, MD: NIAAA, 2000.

"Oprah" (television show). March 26, 2003.

"A Parent's Guide on Teenagers and Drinking." Mothers Against Drunk Driving (MADD). www.madd.org/under21/0,1056,1163,00.html (accessed July 15, 2003).

Parker, K. "What Are Little Girls Made Of? How About Pig Guts and Beer?" *Chicago Tribune,* May 14, 2003, 21.

Sadker, M., and D. Sadker. *Failing at Fairness: How America's Schools Cheat Girls.* New York: Scribners, 1994.

Siegel, D., and M. Hartzell. *Parenting from the Inside Out: How a Deeper Self-Understanding Can Help You Raise Children Who Thrive.* New York: Tarcher Penguin, 2003, 225.

Substance Abuse and Mental Health Services Administration (SAMHSA). "National Household Survey on Drug Abuse Main Findings 1997." Rockville, MD: U.S. Department of Health and Human Services, 1999.

"Thermage: The new non-surgical facelift." Face Facts. CNN.com/2003/health/05/19/nonsurgical.facelift/index.html (accessed May 19, 2003).

Tolman, D. *Dilemmas of Desire: Teenage Girls Talk About Sexuality.* Cambridge, MA: Harvard University Press, 2000.

"Understanding Depression: Depression in Children and Adolescents." University of Michigan Depression Center. www.med.umich.edu/depression/caph.htm (accessed September 14, 2004).

U.S. Department of Education. "Safe and Smart: Making After-School Hours Work for Kids." www.ed.gov/pubs/SafeandSmart/index.html (accessed July 29, 2003).

Wolf, N. *The Beauty Myth.* New York: Anchor Books, 1992.

"Youth, Alcohol, and Other Drugs." National Council on Alcoholism and Drug Dependence. www.ncadd.org/facts/youthalc.html (accessed June 15, 2004).

Chapter 4

American Association of University Women (AAUW). *Gender Gaps: Where Schools Still Fail Our Children.* Washington, DC: AAUW Educational Foundation, 1998.

Cooper, C., J. Denner, and E. Lopez. "Cultural Brokers: Helping Latino Children on Toward Success." *The Future of Children When School Is Out* 9 no. 2 (Fall 1999): 51–56.

Cose, E. "The Black Gender Gap." *Newsweek* (March 3, 2003): 51.

Dietrich, L. C. *Chicana Adolescents.* Westport, CT: Praeger, 1998, 43.

Fordham, S. " 'Those Loud Black Girls': (Black) Women, Silence, and Gender 'Passing' in the Academy." *Rutgers University Anthropology and Education Quarterly* 24 (1): 3-32, 1993.

hooks, b. *Black Looks: Race and Representation.* Boston: South End Press, 1992, 44.

Jacob, I. *My Sisters' Voices: Teenage Girls of Color Speak Out.* New York: Henry Holt & Company, 2002, 19.

Lipson, J. "Sister-to-Sister: Fighting the Code of Silence." *American Association of University Women: Outlook* (Spring 1998): 9.

Potter, J. (ed). "Building Bridges Between Cultures." *WEEA Equity Resource Center Digest* (September 2001): 4.

Samuels, A. "Time to Tell It Like It Is." *Newsweek* (March 3, 2003): 52–55.

Span, P. "It's a Girl's World." *Washington Post Magazine* (June 22, 1997): 11–12.

"Study Finds Link Between Rap Videos and Violence." Parents Television Council. www.parentstv.org/PTC/publications/news/rapstudy.asp (accessed May 29, 2003).

U.S. Department of Commerce, Bureau of the Census. "Current Population Survey." Unpublished tabulations, 2001.

U.S. Department of Education, National Center for Education Statistics. *Dropout Rates in the United States.* July 2001.

Warren-Sams, B. "Mentors Confirm and Enhance Girls' Lives." *WEEA Equity Resource Center Digest* (September 2001): 12–13.

Chapter 5

American Association of University Women (AAUW). *Hostile Hallways: Bullying, Teasing, and Sexual Harassment in School.* Washington, DC: AAUW Educational Foundation, 1998.

American Association of University Women (AAUW). *Hostile Hallways: Bully ing, Teasing, and Sexual Harassment in School.* Washington, DC: AAUW Educational Foundation, 2001.

Brubach, H. "The Athletic Esthetic." *New York Times Magazine* (June 23, 1996): 51.

"Bullying." National Youth Violence Prevention Resource Center. www.safe youth.org/scripts/teens/bullying.asp (accessed September 14, 2004).

"Dating Violence." Child Trends DataBank. www.childtrendsdatabank.org/indicators/66DatingViolence.cfm (accessed March 7, 2003).

Longman, J. "Women Move Closer to Olympic Equality." *New York Times*, August 20, 2000, 1.

Mulrine, A. "Are Boys the Weaker Sex?" *U.S. News and World Report* (July 20, 2001): 40–47.

National Center for Education Statistics. *National Assessment of Educational Progress (NAEP) Reading Assessment, 2000.* Washington, DC: U.S. Department of Education, 2000.

National Center for Education Statistics. *National Assessment of Educational Progress (NAEP) Science Assessment, 2002.* Washington, DC: U.S. Department of Education, 2002.

National Coalition for Women and Girls in Education (NCWGE). *Title IX at 30: A Report Card on Gender Equity.* Washington, DC: NCWGE, 2002, 34.

National Collegiate Athletic Association. *NCAA Year-by-Year Sports Participation 1982–2001. Sports and Recreation Programs of Universities and Colleges 1957–82.* Charts published by the National Federation of State High School Associations in 2001.

Research for Action, Inc. *Girls in the Middle: Working to Succeed in School.* Washington, DC: AAUW Educational Foundation, 1996, 60.

Span, P. "It's a Girl's World." *Washington Post Magazine* (June 22, 1997): 11–12.

Stewart, I. "Girls Take on Sports." *Girls Ink* newsletter (Spring 1997): 5.

U.S. Department of Education (USDOE). *Title IX: 25 Years of Progress.* Washington, DC: USDOE, Office for Civil Rights, 1997, 1.

Wiseman, R. *Queen Bees and Wannabes: Helping Your Daughter Survive Cliques, Gossip, Boyfriends, and Other Realities of Adolescence.* New York: Crown Publishing Group, 2003.

Women's Educational Equity Act Resource Center. *1999 Fact Sheet on Women's and Girls' Educational Equity.* Newton, MA: Education Development Center, 2000.

Chapter 6

American Academy of Child and Adolescent Psychiatry. "Gay and Lesbian Adolescents." www.aacap.org/publications/factsfam/63.htm (accessed March 3, 2003).

Begley, S. "A World of Their Own." *Newsweek* (May 8, 2000): 54.

Green, J. "Out and Organized" *New York Times*, June 13, 1993, sec. 9, 1–7.

Haag, P. *Fitting In, Voices of a Generation: Teenage Girls on Sex, School, and Self.* Washington, DC: AAUW Educational Foundation, 1995, 5.

Hunter, S. "Girls Gone Wild." *Washington Post*, August 29, 2003, C1, C4.

Meadows, S. "Meet the Gamma Girls." *Newsweek* (June 3, 2002): 47.

Mikesell, S. Interview. April 15, 2004.

Ponton, L. "Mind and Body: If She Thinks She's a Lesbian." *Daughters* newsletter. www.daughters.com/0701p9.htm (accessed April 2, 2003).

Stepp, L. Interview. March 20, 2003.

Vail, K. "How Girls Hurt." *American School Board Journal* (August 2002): 14–18.

Wiseman, R. *Queen Bees and Wannabes: Helping Your Daughter Survive Cliques, Gossip, Boyfriends, and Other Realities of Adolescence.* New York: Crown Publishing Group, 2003.

Chapter 7

Adams, B. "Change and Continuity in the U.S. Family Today." *Bangladesh Journal of Sociology* (1998).

Association of Family and Conciliation Courts. *Rights of Children of Divorce.* Madison, WI: AFCC, 1998.

Brumberg, J. *The Body Project.* New York: Random House, 1997.

Edelman, H. *Motherless Daughter.* New York: Addison Wesley, 1994.

Ganahl, J. "Single-Minded, Even a Daughter Can Want to Be Just Like Dad." *San Francisco Chronicle* (June 16, 2002): E1.

Hetherington, E. M. "Virginia Longitudinal Study of Divorce." In *For Better or for Worse: Divorce Reconsidered*. New York: W. W. Norton and Company, 2002.

Kelly, J. "Q & A with Joe Kelly." *The MentorGirl Voice* newsletter. www.men torgirls.org/voice/voice_rm2_Jan2k3.html (accessed September 25, 2003).

Mann, J. *The Difference: Growing Up Female in America*. New York: Warner Books, 1994, 270.

Peterson, K. S. "Kids of Divorced Parents Straddle a Divided World." *USA Today*, July 13, 2003.

Siegel, D., and M. Hartzell. *Parenting from the Inside Out: How a Deeper Self-Understanding Can Help You Raise Children Who Thrive*. New York: Tarcher Penguin, 2003, 225.

Snyderman, N. *Girl in the Mirror: Mothers and Daughters in the Years of Adolescence*. New York: Hyperion, 2002, 5, 12–13.

"Ten Tips for Dads of Daughters." Dads and Daughters. www.dadsanddaugh ters.org/library/tentips.html (accessed March 20, 2003).

Chapter 8

Asian Women United of California. *Making Waves: An Anthology of Writings by and About Asian American Women*. Boston: Beacon Press, 1989, 198.

Clinton, H. R. Speech given at the 150th anniversary of the first women's rights convention, Seneca Falls, NY, July 16, 1998.

Friedan, B. *The Feminine Mystique*. New York: Dell Publishing Company, 1963.

Harrison, C. "From the Home to the House: The Changing Role of Women in American Society." U.S. Department of State International Information Programs. http://usinfo.state.gov/journals/itsv/0597/ijse/kitch.htm (accessed September 1, 2003).

Lange, A. "The Family Gap: Do Mothers Earn Less?" *The Park Place Economist* (April 2001): 9.

Mann, J. *The Difference: Growing Up Female in America*. New York: Warner Books, 1994, 9.

Snyderman, N. *Girl in the Mirror: Mothers and Daughters in the Years of Adolescence*. New York: Hyperion, 2002, 23, 50–51, 57.

Taylor, M. D. *Roll of Thunder, Hear My Cry*. New York: Bantam Books, 1976, vii.

Wolf, N. *The Beauty Myth*. New York: Anchor Books, 1992, 19.

Chapter 9

American Psychological Association Task Force on Adolescent Girls: Strengths and Stresses. "A New Look at Adolescent Girls." American Psychological Association. Gender. www.apa.org/pi/cyf/adolesgirls.html (accessed August 6, 2003).

Lerner, H. *The Dance of Connection*. New York: Harper Collins, 2001.

Siegel, D., and M. Hartzell. *Parenting from the Inside Out: How a Deeper Self-Understanding Can Help You Raise Children Who Thrive*. New York: Tarcher Penguin, 2003, 225.

Chapter 10

Foster, D. "The Disease Is Adolescence." *Rolling Stone* (December 9, 1993): 55–60, 78.

Grogan, T., and L. Bechtel. "Improving Gender Relationships in School." *Responsive Classroom* newsletter. www.responsiveclassroom.org/newsletter/15_1NL_1.asp (accessed October 1, 2003).

Mann, J. *The Difference: Growing Up Female in America*. New York: Warner Books, 1994, 281, 290.

McClure, A. "Wimpy Boys and Macho Girls: Gender Equity at the Crossroads." National Council of Teachers of English. www.ncte.org/pubs/journals/ej/articles/108472.htm (accessed September 6, 2003).

Nieken, J. "Boys Are Better Than Girls: Adolescent Gender Socialization in North America." http://rubi-con.org/nieken/writ/gendersocialization.html (accessed March 2003).

Stepp, L. Interview. March 20, 2003.

Stowe, H. B. "Letter to Her Twin Daughters." www.ovalocity.com/html/quotes/experience.html (accessed June 17, 2004).

Will, G. "Disconnected Youth." *Washington Post*, September 21, 2003, B7.

Winik, L. W. "Parade's Special Intelligence Report." *Parade* (March 2, 2003): 16.

Index

Adams, Bert, 161
Adolescent boys, xii, 192, 193, 199
  competition, 5
  performance, 14
  sisters and, 200
Adolescent development, 26, 86
Adolescent girls. *See also specific issues*
  girls of color, 79–93
  imagining life as a boy, 202
  as market group, 32
Adult supervision, 66–67, 68, 69. *See also*
  Parenting skills
Advertising, 22, 31. *See also* Media
  girls of color, 84
African-American girls, 41–42, 82, 83.
  See also Girls of color
  "attitude," 87, 88
  social versus intellectual issues,
    88
Aggression, 4–8, 178
  passive-aggressive, 6, 124
  self-assertion, 6
Ahrons, Constance, 158
Alcohol, 67, 69–73
"Alpha girls," 98, 121

American Academy of Child and
  Adolescent Psychiatry, 214
American Association of University Women
  (AAUW), 26, 60, 85, 87, 103
American Psychological Association Task
  Force on Adolescent Girls, 180
Anger, 4, 5, 8, 178
  depression and, 73–74
Anorexia nervosa, 27, 218. *See also* Eating
  disorders
Anorexia Nervosa and Related Eating
  Orders, Inc. (ANRED), 26
Asian-Americans girls, 82, 89–90, 165. *See*
  also Girls of color
Association of Family and Conciliation
  Courts, 159
Athletic abilities and sports, 43, 110–13, 182,
  186
  college scholarships, 112
  role models, 111
"Attitude," 87, 88
Authenticity
  daughters and, 174–76
  freedom of expression, 196
  parents and, 15–17, 134

About the Authors

Susan Morris Shaffer is currently the deputy director and director of gender equity programs at the Mid-Atlantic Equity Center. Shaffer is nationally recognized for her work in the development of comprehensive technical assistance and training programs on educational equity and multicultural gender-related issues. She has authored or coauthored several publications related to gender equity, mathematics and science education, women's history, multicultural education, and disability. She has managed a number of grants from the U.S. Department of Education and has spent more than 30 years teaching and working in public schools. Shaffer holds an undergraduate degree in history and a graduate degree in education from the University of California, Berkeley.

Linda Perlman Gordon, M.S.W., M.Ed., is a clinical social worker, family therapist, and trained mediator. She has directed a court-mandated seminar for divorcing parents and, as a member of the Montgomery County Divorce Roundtable, developed the Supervised Visitation Program for Montgomery County, Maryland. Gordon has been invited to several judicial institutes to speak on issues related to children and divorce. She is a graduate of the Family Therapy Practice Center and has advanced degrees in social work and education. Gordon has taught seminars on the subject of families and developed programs concerning mental health issues for children. She has a private psychotherapy practice in the Washington, D.C., area treating individuals, couples, and families.

Gordon and Shaffer are coauthors of *Why Boys Don't Talk—and Why It Matters: A Parent's Survival Guide to Connecting with Your Teen* (McGraw-Hill, 2005) and *Mom, Can I Move Back in with You?: A Survival Guide for Parents of Twenty-Somethings* (Jeremy P. Tarcher/Putnam, 2004). As a result of this work, they have spoken to parent groups and educators nationally and have been the subject of numerous interviews and articles in print, radio, and television. They were invited to participate at the White House Conference on Teenagers.

For more information, log onto their website, www.parentingroadmaps .com.